How to Use This Book

Look for these special features in this book:

SIDEBARS, **CHARTS**, **GRAPHS**, and original **MAPS** expand your understanding of what's being discussed—and also make useful sources for classroom reports.

FAQs answer common **F**requently **A**sked **Q**uestions about people, places, and things.

WOW FACTORS offer "Who knew?" facts to keep you thinking.

TRAVEL GUIDE gives you tips on exploring the state—either in person or right from your chair!

PROJECT ROOM provides fun ideas for school assignments and incredible research projects. Plus, there's a guide to primary sources—what they are and how to cite them.

Please note: All statistics are as up-to-date as possible at the time of publication. Population data is taken from the 2010 census.

Consultants: Sarah Chadima, Geologist, South Dakota Geological Survey; Herbert Hoover, Professor Emeritus, University of South Dakota; William Loren Katz; Steven J. Bucklin, Professor of History, University of South Dakota

Book production by The Design Lab

Library of Congress Cataloging-in-Publication Data
Burgan, Michael.
 South Dakota / by Michael Burgan. — Revised edition.
   pages cm. — (America the beautiful. Third series)
 Includes bibliographical references and index.
 ISBN 978-0-531-28293-9 (library binding : alk. paper)
 1. South Dakota—Juvenile literature. I. Title.
 F651.3.B87 2014
 974.5—dc23   2013044803

1 2 3 4 5 6 7 8 9 10 R 24 23 22 21 20 19 18 17 16 15

AMERICA ★ THE ★ BEAUTIFUL

South Dakota

BY MICHAEL BURGAN

Third Series, Revised Edition

Children's Press®
An Imprint of Scholastic Inc.
New York ★ Toronto ★ London ★ Auckland ★ Sydney
Mexico City ★ New Delhi ★ Hong Kong
Danbury, Connecticut

CONTENTS

N W E S

NORTH DAKOTA

Fort Sisseton Historic State Park

Motorcycle Museum & Hall of Fame

Grand

Moreau

Missouri

ABERDEEN

WATERTOWN

South Dakota Air and Space Museum

G r e a t   Lake Oahe   P l a i n s

South Dakota Art Museum

Big Sioux

Black Hills National Forest

Cheyenne

SOUTH DAKOTA

James

Great Plains Zoo

Mount Rushmore

PIERRE

South Dakota State Capitol

RAPID CITY

CHAMBERLAIN

SIOUX FALLS

Custer State Park

White

Akta Lakota Museum & Cultural Center

Badlands National Park

Missouri

South Dakota Hall of Fame

YANKTON

Jewel Cave National Monument

USS South Dakota Battleship Memorial

NEBRASKA

QUICK FACTS

State capital: Pierre
Largest city: Sioux Falls
Total area: 77,116 square miles (199,730 sq km)
Highest point: Harney Peak, 7,242 feet (2,207 m), in Pennington County
Lowest point: Big Stone Lake, 966 feet (294 m), in Roberts County

0   40
Miles

Welcome to South Dakota!

HOW DID SOUTH DAKOTA GET ITS NAME?

Almost 300 years ago, a group of Native Americans headed west out of Minnesota searching for new hunting grounds. In their language, the word for "friend" was *koda* or *kola*. Some of these people called themselves Dakota, meaning "alliance of friends." Over time, European fur traders and explorers came to the native lands, located along the Missouri River and other nearby waterways. In 1861, the United States named this region the Dakota Territory. Twenty-eight years later, two states were formed from the territory: North Dakota and South Dakota.

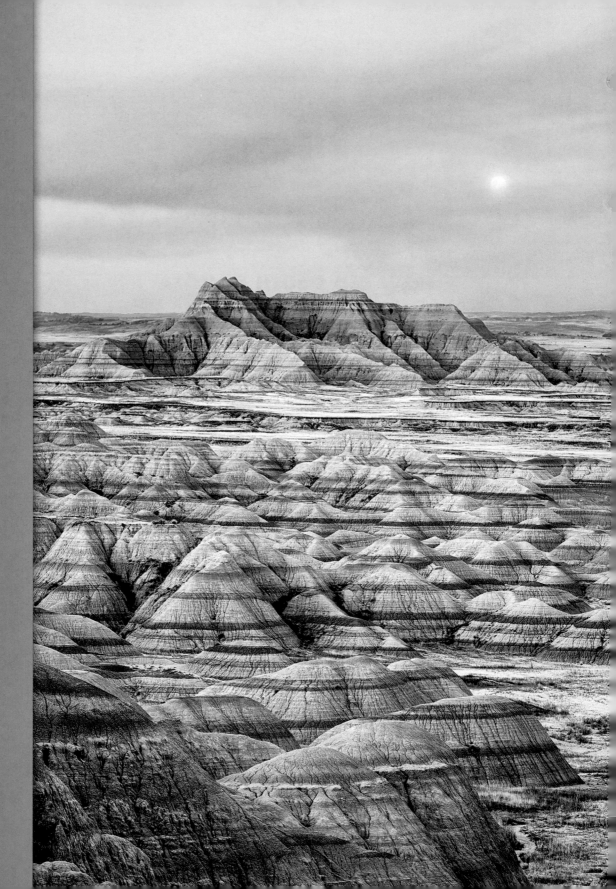

READ ABOUT

Rock formations
at Badlands
National Park

CHAPTER ONE

LAND

★

SOUTH DAKOTA HAS BEEN CALLED "THE LAND OF INFINITE VARIETY." Infinite, or limitless, may not be completely accurate. Still, with its sprawling, flat plains, rolling hills, broad river valleys, and majestic mountains, South Dakota boasts a wide range of natural beauty. South Dakota is the 17th-largest state, with a total area of 77,116 square miles (199,730 square kilometers). Its highest point is 7,242 feet (2,207 meters) at Harney Peak in the Black Hills. Its lowest spot is 966 feet (294 m) at Big Stone Lake, in the northeast corner of the state.

FAQ

Q8 WHAT IS THE LARGEST FOSSIL EVER FOUND IN SOUTH DAKOTA?

A8 In 1990, explorer Sue Hendrickson was looking for dinosaur bones in the Black Hills of South Dakota. She uncovered the largest, most complete skeleton of a *T. rex* ever found. The *T. rex* skeleton, now called Sue, is on display at Chicago's Field Museum.

WORD TO KNOW

glaciers *slow-moving masses of ice*

ANCIENT WATER AND ICE

More than 300 million years ago, seas covered most of what is now the central United States, including South Dakota. At one time, huge sea turtles and other now-extinct water creatures lived in the region. Over millions of years, the seas receded and then returned several times. After the land was finally dry, dinosaurs and ancient mammals lived in today's South Dakota. These included *Tyrannosaurus rex*, one of the largest meat eaters ever to walk the earth. Fossils of these dinosaurs and other ancient creatures are still being uncovered in the state today.

About 2 million years ago, huge continental ice sheets began to drift southward over North America. These **glaciers** shaped the land of eastern South Dakota by crushing and scraping the land's surface in their path. The last glaciers melted away about 10,000 years ago, leaving

South Dakota Geo-Facts

Along with the state's geographical highlights, this chart ranks South Dakota's land, water, and total area compared to all other states.

Total area; rank . . . . . 77,116 square miles (199,730 sq km); 17th
Land; rank . . . . 75,811 square miles (196,350 sq km); 16th
Water; rank . . . . 1,305 square miles (3,380 sq km); 29th
Inland water; rank . . . . . 1,305 square miles (3,380 sq km); 17th
Geographic center . . . . Hughes, 8 miles (13 km) northeast of Pierre
Latitude . . . . 42°29'30" N to 45°56' N
Longitude . . . . .98°28'33" W to 104°3' W
Highest point . . . . .Harney Peak, 7,242 feet (2,207 m), in Pennington County
Lowest point . . . . Big Stone Lake, 966 feet (294 m), in Roberts County
Largest city . . . . Sioux Falls
Longest river . . . . .Missouri River

Source: U.S. Census Bureau, 2010 census

Rhode Island, the smallest U.S. state, could fit inside South Dakota 49 times.

A researcher works on a 25,000-year-old mammoth skeleton at Hot Springs.

sand, gravel, and clay behind. The melting ice also created lakes and rivers.

In western South Dakota, the land was further shaped by ancient oceans and **erosion**. Some of the rocks on the surface are made up of materials that once lay on ocean bottoms. In other areas, erosion has deposited and carved land out of rocks.

LAND REGIONS

South Dakota sits almost in the middle of the Great Plains, a mostly flat, grassy region that stretches from northern Mexico to the heart of Canada. In the United States, the Great Plains cuts through the center of the country, roughly halfway between the Rocky Mountains and the Mississippi River.

The landscape of South Dakota features three main regions: the Central Lowlands, the Great Plains, and the Black Hills.

WORD TO KNOW

erosion *the wearing away of land by water, ice, wind, and other factors*

South Dakota Topography

Use the color-coded elevation chart to see on the map South Dakota's high points (dark red to orange) and low points (green to dark green). Elevation is measured as the distance above or below sea level.

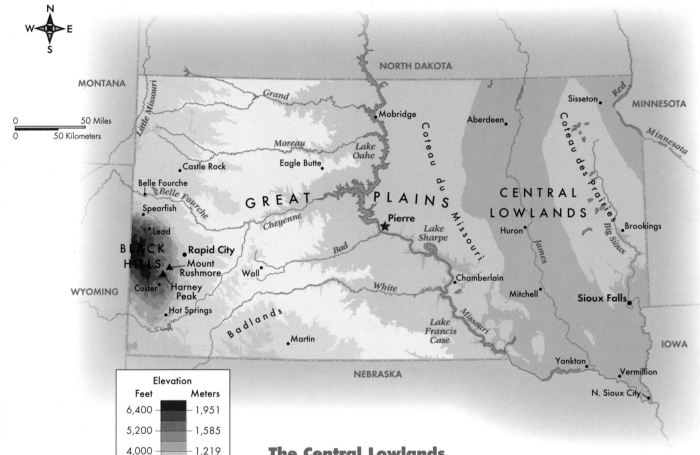

Elevation	
Feet	Meters
6,400	1,951
5,200	1,585
4,000	1,219
2,800	853
1,600	488

WORD TO KNOW

plateau *an elevated part of the earth with steep slopes*

The Central Lowlands

The Central Lowlands region sits in eastern South Dakota. A large part of the region is the James River Lowland, a low-lying plain. Another part of this region is actually a **plateau** that rises about 2,000 feet (610 m) above sea level. Called the Coteau des Prairies (French for "slope of the prairies"), this plateau is about 200 miles (322 km) long and 100 miles (161 km) wide. Hills dot the Central Lowlands, an area that features some of the best farmland in the country.

Horses grazing in Jones County, in the central part of the state

The Great Plains

This region of South Dakota begins east of the Missouri River and stretches west, covering almost two-thirds of the state. It includes an interesting feature, the Missouri River Trench, where the land drops suddenly from a plateau to a narrow valley along the river. The Great Plains region is covered with grasslands that provide food for herds of cattle, sheep, and other grazing animals.

In the southwestern part of the Great Plains region is a dry stretch of land with deep canyons, towering spires, and flat-topped tables. The Sioux Indians called it *mako sica*—"land bad." Today, it is called the Badlands. The term *badlands* refers to any dry, heavily eroded land.

SEE IT HERE!

BADLANDS NATIONAL PARK

Ancient oceans helped form the layers of rock that make up the Badlands. Rivers and rain then eroded the soft layers of rock, shaping the steep, jagged cliffs called buttes. Even today, rain can cause a butte to fall to the ground. The U.S. government first recognized the unique beauty of the Badlands in 1929 and in 1978 made it into a national park. Within the park are fossils dating back more than 79 million years.

Hikers on Harney Peak in the Black Hills

The Black Hills

Look at a map of the United States, and you'll see the Rocky Mountains cutting north to south across the western part of the country. To the east of this range are the Black Hills, which formed at almost the same time as the Rockies. These "hills," which reach more than 7,000 feet (2,100 m) high, have been called a mini version of the mighty Rockies. The mountains contain gold, lead, and other mineral resources.

From the air, the rocks of the Black Hills look very much like an oblong archery target. Rings of different rocks dip away from the center. The most dramatic ring on the outside of the target is called the Great Hogback. These series of steep slopes reminded early explorers of the ridges on the back of a razorback hog. At the Needles, another region in the Black Hills, rock climbers test their skills on the thin, sharp spires.

THE MISSOURI AND OTHER RIVERS

On its way from Montana to the Mississippi River, the 2,341-mile-long (3,767 km) Missouri River flows through South Dakota. For much of its journey through the state, the Missouri River almost divides South Dakota in half, separating east and west. Then the river takes a turn east and forms part of the border between South Dakota and Nebraska. In the eastern half of the state, the major rivers flow north to south, including the James and the Big Sioux. West of the Missouri, the rivers flow primarily from west to east. These include the Grand, Moreau, Cheyenne, Bad, and White rivers.

CLIMATE

South Dakota has cold winters and warm summers. The southeast is the wettest part of the state. North of this region, less **precipitation** falls and the summers are a little shorter. In the west, the air tends to be drier. In the Black Hills, weather conditions change quickly, depending on elevation and location. South Dakota is generally very windy. Even on a sunny day, the constant stiff winds can make it hard to walk or open a car door.

In the spring and summer, thunderstorms and tornadoes are common in South Dakota.

In 1968, winds of up to 150 miles per hour (241 kph) blew through parts of eastern South Dakota for 20 minutes. That's as strong as an extremely damaging hurricane.

WORD TO KNOW

precipitation *all water that falls to the earth, including rain, sleet, hail, snow, dew, fog, or mist*

Weather Report

This chart shows record temperatures (high and low) for the state, as well as average temperatures (July and January) and average annual precipitation.

Record high temperature . . . . 120°F (49°C) at Gann Valley on July 5, 1936 and at Fort Pierre on July 15, 2006
Record low temperature . . . . –58°F (–50°C) at McIntosh on February 17, 1936
Average July temperature, Sioux Falls . . . . 73°F (23°C)
Average January temperature, Sioux Falls . . . . . . 17°F (–8°C)
Average yearly precipitation, Sioux Falls . . . 16 inches (41 cm)

Source: National Climatic Data Center, NESDIS, NOAA, U.S. Department of Commerce

A bison roams a snow-covered plain in South Dakota.

The town of Lead holds the state record for annual snowfall. In 1997, it got 324 inches (823 centimeters)—that's 27 feet!

The winter brings snowstorms and, on average, three full-blown blizzards a year. In 1888, during one of the worst blizzards in the state's history, dozens of schoolchildren died as they walked home from school and got caught in the storm.

PLANT LIFE

Vast grasslands once blanketed South Dakota. Prairie grass up to 6 feet (1.8 m) tall covered the southeastern corner of South Dakota. Farmland has since replaced much of this grass. The height of the prairie grass decreases as you move from east to west across the state. About two-thirds of the state, starting east of the Missouri River, is called the short- and mid-grass region. Cattle, sheep, and other livestock graze on blue grama and wheatgrass that grow there.

The state flower, the American pasque, grows all across the state, most commonly in the east. Prairie rose and goldenrod also brighten the plains.

Only about 4 percent of South Dakota's land is covered with trees. Nearly all of this woodland is located in the Black Hills. Many kinds of pines grow there, along with the Black Hills spruce—the state tree. Deciduous, or leaf-bearing, trees are not as common as evergreens in South Dakota, but cottonwood, black walnut, and ash do grow in the state. Maple and scrub oak trees are common in eastern South Dakota.

A prairie coneflower growing among horsemint in Wind Cave National Park

South Dakota National Park Areas

This map shows some of South Dakota's national parks, monuments, preserves, and other areas protected by the National Park Service.

	National Park area
NHS	National Historic Site
NHT	National Historic Trail
NMEM	National Memorial
NM	National Monument
NP	National Park
NRR	National Recreational River

0   50 Miles
0   50 Kilometers

FAQ ★ ★ ★

Q: WHY ARE BISON SOMETIMES CALLED BUFFALO?

A: The correct name for the shaggy beast is bison—true buffalo are found only in Asia and Europe. But early settlers thought bison looked like buffalo, and the name has been used ever since.

ANIMAL LIFE

A wide variety of wildlife live on South Dakota's prairies, plains, and mountains. Deer and pronghorn thrive, as do elk, mountain lions, and wolves. The coyote is the state animal, and sometimes South Dakota is called the Coyote State. Huge herds of bison, often called buffalo,

ENDANGERED ANIMALS

South Dakotans are trying to protect animals in danger of becoming extinct. The Eskimo curlew and the majestic whooping crane are two birds in danger because they have lost their habitat. Fish on the state's **endangered** species list include the pallid sturgeon and the banded killifish. Two insects in danger are the American burying beetle and the Dakota skipper, a type of butterfly.

The whooping crane is an endangered species that is native to South Dakota.

once roamed the state, but their numbers fell sharply in the 19th century, and they almost became extinct. Today, bison herds again live on preserves in the west and on ranches across the state. Mountain goats and wild burros live in the Black Hills. Small mammals in the state include jackrabbits, prairie dogs, and squirrels.

Bald eagles nest in South Dakota each year. More common birds are pheasants, ducks, geese, hawks, owls, and finches. South Dakota has just one native poisonous snake—the prairie rattler. Most are found west of the Missouri River. In the state's lakes, rivers, and streams live fish such as walleye, bass, trout, and carp.

WORD TO KNOW

endangered *at risk of becoming extinct*

Prairie dogs

In 2012, the conservation group **Ducks Unlimited** restored or protected more than 10,000 acres (4,000 hectares) of South Dakota wetlands and nearby areas.

These pronghorn fawns in Custer State Park are among many animals protected in South Dakota's natural areas.

HUMANS AND THE ENVIRONMENT

When European American settlers first came to South Dakota, they began to plow up the prairies to create farmland. By the 21st century, more than 40 percent of South Dakota's native prairie had disappeared. Wetlands have disappeared at almost the same rate. As these environments are lost, the plants and animals that live there find it hard to survive.

In recent years, South Dakotans have worked to save some of the remaining prairies and wetlands. Ranchers move livestock around from year to year, so the grass they graze on has a chance to regrow. As new buildings are constructed, developers set aside some land as wildlife habitat. Farmers plant grass and trees on the edges of their farms to provide new homes for animals of all kinds.

The rows of trees found along many South Dakota farms are called windbreaks, or **shelterbelts**. The trees help pre-

MINI-BIO

LINDA M. HASSELSTROM: WRITER, RANCHER, ENVIRONMENTALIST

Linda Hasselstrom (1943–) grew up on a ranch in Hermosa, near the Black Hills. After graduating from the University of South Dakota, she left the state for a time before returning home to the family ranch. Her experiences on the ranch led her to write books and poems about life on the Great Plains. Living close to the land helped her realize how important it is to save the grasslands and the plants and animals that live there. For a time, Hasselstrom worked with environmental groups, but she decided writing was a more effective way to show others the need to preserve the Great Plains. She now operates a writing center on her ranch.

? Want to know more? Visit www.factsfor now.scholastic.com and enter the keywords **South Dakota**.

Modern wind turbines, shown near a wooden windmill, help generate energy in South Dakota.

vent the wind and water from carrying away the soil, keeping farmland healthy.

South Dakotans are also looking for ways to create energy that will not pollute the environment the way burning coal and oil do. In 2003, the Wind Energy Center in Hyde County, the state's first wind farm, was built. Today, South Dakota leads the nation in energy produced by wind power, with more than 22 percent of the state's electricity generated by wind **turbines**. Four dams on the Missouri River provide most of the state's power from water. Hydroelectric power accounts for about half of the electricity used in the state.

WORD TO KNOW

turbines *machines for making power through the rotation of blades powered by wind, water, or steam*

READ ABOUT

Early hunters crossing the Bering Strait from Asia

▲ **c. 10,000 BCE**

Native people hunt mammoths in what is now South Dakota

c. 500 CE

Mound Builders arrive in South Dakota

c. 1000

Pre-Arikaras arrive in the region

CHAPTER TWO

FIRST PEOPLE

★

SCIENTISTS BELIEVE THAT THE ANCESTORS OF THE FIRST SOUTH DAKOTANS TRAVELED TO NORTH AMERICA FROM ASIA. Some people may have walked over a land bridge that once connected what are now Russia and Alaska. Others may have come by boat. From their landing points, these first settlers spread out over North America.

Arikara pottery

▲ **c. 1300–mid-1500s**
Arikaras arrive in South Dakota

c. 1600
Arikaras begin trading for European goods

mid-1700s
Sioux come to South Dakota from Minnesota

In the area that is now South Dakota, early peoples hunted bison for food and clothing.

WORD TO KNOW

archaeologists *people who study the remains of past human societies*

EARLY HUNTERS AND GATHERERS

The first people to reach today's South Dakota used sharp, stone-tipped spears to kill prey such as mammoths and mastodons. The animals provided food, and hunters turned the bones into tools. On the Pine Ridge Indian Reservation in southwestern South Dakota, **archaeologists** have found evidence that early hunters killed mammoths there about 12,000 years ago.

During the next several thousand years, different groups of people came to South Dakota to hunt. They were nomadic, walking from place to place in search of game. By about 8000 BCE, mammoths and mastodons were extinct, and bison became the main food for people in today's South Dakota. People hunted bison both by spearing them and by chasing them off cliffs. They also killed smaller animals and gathered wild plants such as vegetables and berries.

FIRST VILLAGES

Around 500 CE, people from the south began to move into today's South Dakota. They are sometimes called the Mound Builders, because they buried their dead under huge mounds of earth. Later Mound Builders, called Mississippians, erected their most important buildings atop the mounds.

In South Dakota, Mound Builders settled in small villages along rivers such as the Big Sioux and the Missouri. They hunted, fished, and farmed, raising corn, squash, and beans.

PRE-ARIKARA

Starting around the year 1000, people now called Pre-Arikaras moved into South Dakota from Minnesota. They built much larger villages than the Mound Builders had, and they erected tall, wooden fences called palisades around their communities. The palisades were designed to keep out invading enemies. Pre-Arikaras made their homes, or lodges, out of a mixture of grass and clay. Wooden posts held up the ceilings, which were made of grass mats and branches. As many as 20 family members might have shared one lodge.

Pre-Arikaras regularly traded with other Native Americans. They obtained stones such as flint and quartz—which they used as arrow and spear points—most likely by trading extra food they had grown.

ARIKARA

The Arikara people moved into South Dakota between 1300 and the mid-1500s, settling along the Missouri and Grand rivers. Like Pre-Arikaras, they farmed and lived in earthen lodges. Sometimes they also used tipis, cone-shaped tents made with bison skins.

SEE IT HERE!

A VILLAGE FROM THE PAST

In 1910, a college student from Mitchell uncovered the remains of a village that was about 1,000 years old. Since then, archaeologists have worked at the site, learning more about the Native people who once lived there. Today, the dig site is the heart of the Mitchell Prehistoric Indian Village. A huge building covers the dig site where archaeologists continue to work. Visitors can see traces of the village. A separate museum contains a model of an earth lodge and provides details about the lives of Pre-Arikaras.

Arikara man

Native American Peoples

(Before European Contact)

This map shows the general area of Native American peoples before European settlers arrived.

Corn was so central to Arikara life that the people sometimes called themselves "corn eaters."

In Arikara villages, women were the farmers. In addition to corn, squash, and beans, they also raised pumpkins and tobacco. They traded extra crops to the Lakota Sioux, Cheyenne, and other nations for animal hides and, later, horses. Starting around 1600, Arikaras also traded for goods from Europe, including metal pots and guns. The first European traders and explorers had come to North America in the early 16th century.

Members of the Dakota people, who settled in the eastern part of the region

SIOUX

While Arikaras thrived in their villages, Native people from Minnesota sometimes came to South Dakota to hunt and fish. In the mid-18th century, they began settling in South Dakota. Ojibwa people called these communities *Nadowe Su*, which means "little rattle." The name refers to the rattle of a rattlesnake. Eventually, the name of the newcomers was shortened to Sioux.

The Sioux eventually divided into three main groups: Dakota, Nakota, and Lakota. The Dakota people settled in the southeastern part of South Dakota. They included four groups: Mdewakantons, Wahpekutes, Sissetons, and Wahpetons. To the northwest of them lived the Nakota people, who were divided into Yanktons, the Upper and

In winter, Sioux hunters sometimes used snowshoes in their pursuit of bison.

To the Sioux, even a bison's stomach was useful. It was cleaned out and used as a sack to store and carry water.

Lower Yanktonais, and Assiniboines. In western South Dakota, near the Black Hills, lived the Lakota people. They were divided into Oglalas, Brulés, Minneconjous, Sans Arcs, Two Kettles, Blackfoot Sioux, and Hunkpapas.

Sioux were expert hunters. Bison was their main prey, but they also hunted bear, elk, and deer. They used almost every part of the bison for their daily needs. They turned the hides into robes, shirts, belts, and tipi covers. They made tools from the bones, and the animals' horns served as cups and spoons. For hundreds of years, Sioux hunted bison on foot, but in the mid-1700s, they obtained horses from other Native American nations, which made hunting easier.

There were differences in the ways the three main groups lived. Dakotas had large lodges where some people lived while raising corn or gathering nuts and berries. The majority of Nakotas lived in permanent villages year-round. Lakotas were the most nomadic of the Sioux nations, often following herds of bison across the plains. In winter, they settled in camps, where they prepared for the next hunting season. Hunters from all groups lived in tipis as they traveled.

In Sioux society, men spent most of their time hunting game, trading with other tribes, or waging war. Men, especially Lakota men, were expert riders and skilled with a bow and arrow. In battle, Sioux fighters valued bravery and skill.

Sioux women took charge of the family and the camps. They owned a family's tipi and set it up after each move. Women also butchered bison for their meat and tanned their hides so they could be used for clothing. Sioux women raised crops and gathered nuts, seeds, and berries for meals.

As they went about their daily lives, Sioux felt the presence of many spirits.

ELLA DELORIA: ANTHROPOLOGIST

In her Yankton Sioux family, Ella Deloria (1889–1971) was called Apetu Waste Win—"Beautiful Day Woman." Deloria left her Yankton reservation and spent time with the Lakota before becoming an **anthropologist**. As part of her work, she visited South Dakota reservations and gathered stories about Sioux history. That research was the core of her 1932 book Dakota Texts, which explains Sioux culture and language to the outside world. Throughout her career, she met her goal of making "the Dakota people understandable, as human beings, to the white people who dealt with them."

? **Want to know more?** Visit www.factsfornow.scholastic.com and enter the keywords **South Dakota**.

WORD TO KNOW

anthropologist *a person who studies the development of human cultures*

FAQ

Q: WHAT WERE WINTER COUNTS?
A: A winter count served as the Lakota's visual calendar and history book. It was made of animal hides with pictures drawn on them. Each year, the calendar's keeper drew an image that represented important events from the past year.

Picture Yourself . . .

Growing Up in a Lakota Camp

As a child, you stayed close to your mother as she searched for food and set up the family tipi. But now you are older. You are expected to search for food, too, and to gather firewood. If you are a boy, at about age 12 or 13 you go with your father and other men to learn the skills of a warrior. You've been riding and racing horses for several years already, and you've learned to shoot a bow and arrow. If you are a girl, you learn how to skin bison, sew, and set up tipis.

Meat drying outside tipis on the plains

Some spirits helped humans, while others represented evil. To Sioux, the universe was the creation of Wakan Tanka Tunkasila, the Great (or Holy) Spirit, Grandfather. All people, animals, and plants were connected through the creator. Even rocks and other nonliving things were *wakan*, meaning "holy."

Lakotas honored Wakan Tanka Tunkasila and other spirits. They also believed certain animals had special powers or offered special services to humans. Bison, for example, were sacred because they provided everything the Sioux needed to live. Bison skulls were used in some religious ceremonies. Bears were thought to show Lakotas which roots could be used to cure illnesses.

To stay in touch with the spirit world, the Sioux relied on medicine men, who were thought to have been born knowing the nature of what was sacred. Learning from the medicine men who came before them, Sioux gained the skills to understand the spirits and what they wanted humans to do.

The vision quest was a key part of a Sioux's spiritual life. On a vision quest, a person—usually a man—went

A portrait of Blue Medicine, a medicine man of the eastern Dakotas, by painter George Catlin

MODERN-DAY MEDICINE MAN

In the 19th and 20th centuries, the U.S. government tried to destroy the Sioux's ancient spiritual beliefs and practices. But some medicine men, such as Wallace Black Elk (1921–2004) secretly learned the old ways. Black Elk grew up on the Rosebud Reservation, where he spent time with a medicine man named Nicholas Black Elk. Once Wallace Black Elk mastered these skills, he shared Lakota beliefs in a book, interviews, and lectures. He pushed for a law, passed in 1978, that gave all Native Americans the freedom to follow their traditional spiritual practices. He believed non-Sioux could also benefit from learning the ancient wisdom of his people.

out alone onto a high hill for up to four days. He went without food and water, waiting for the spirits to send a message. The spirit might appear in the form of an animal or bird. Once the person had a vision, he returned home and discussed what he had seen or heard with a medicine man, who helped him understand it. With the wisdom gained from vision quests, Sioux believed they would lead better lives.

32

READ ABOUT

Trappers setting out
for a beaver hunt

1700s
A smallpox epidemic
kills thousands of
Arikaras

1743 ▲
The La Vérendrye
brothers are the first
known European
explorers in South
Dakota

1804
The Lewis and
Clark expedition
travels through South
Dakota on the way to
the Pacific Ocean

EXPLORATION AND SETTLEMENT

CHAPTER THREE

EXPLORATION AND SETTLEMENT

★

IN THE 17TH CENTURY, FRENCH FUR TRADERS AND TRAPPERS WORKED NEAR THE UPPER MISSISSIPPI RIVER AND THE GREAT LAKES. Through trade, their goods reached the Arikara people of South Dakota. Then, starting early in the 18th century, French traders themselves came to South Dakota, and European settlement slowly followed.

▲ **early 1800s**
The fur trade thrives in South Dakota

1856
Sioux Falls, the first permanent European American town in South Dakota, is founded

1861
The U.S. government creates the Dakota Territory

European Exploration of South Dakota

The colored arrows on this map show the routes taken by explorers between 1743 and 1806.

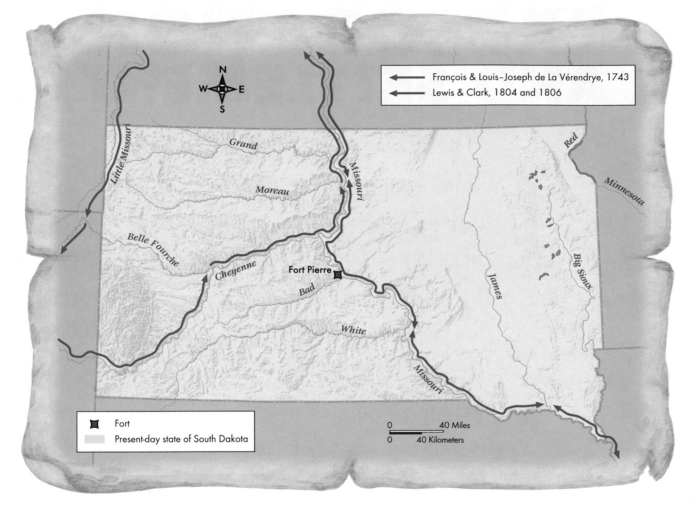

François & Louis-Joseph de La Vérendrye, 1743

Lewis & Clark, 1804 and 1806

Fort

Present-day state of South Dakota

0   40 Miles

0   40 Kilometers

Fort Pierre

EUROPEANS ARRIVE

French trappers working along the Minnesota River might have been the first Europeans to enter South Dakota. By 1701, the French had made a map of the region around the Big Sioux River. The first documented proof of Europeans in South Dakota came in 1743. Two French Canadian brothers, Louis-Joseph and François de La Vérendrye, led a small party south from what is now Canada. Along the

The La Vérendrye brothers explored the region in 1743.

way, they buried two metal plates that their father had made in Quebec, Canada. The dates and the names of several of the explorers were scratched into the metal. The plates were discovered in the 20th century.

For decades after the La Vérendrye explorations, few Europeans came to South Dakota. Still, the presence of Europeans in North America was already spelling disaster for some Native people in today's South Dakota. During the 18th century, the Arikara population reached a height of about 30,000. But diseases, such as smallpox, that Europeans brought with them to North America began to have a deadly effect. The Arikara Nation and neighboring groups had no natural defenses against these illnesses. Arikaras died by the thousands.

A Labrador retriever named Ben helped uncover some of South Dakota's history—he found one of the La Vérendrye plates in 1995.

WORDS TO KNOW

allies *people who are on the same side in a conflict*

expedition *a trip for the purpose of exploration*

After the British defeated the French and their Indian **allies** in the French and Indian War (1754–1763), France lost most of its colonial lands in North America to Great Britain. But the British focused on their existing trade in Canada instead of exploring lands farther west. The Revolutionary War between Great Britain and the 13 American colonies further cut down travel and trade in the west.

At the end of the American Revolution in 1783, South Dakota was part of the vast Louisiana Territory, which stretched west from the Mississippi River all the way to the Rocky Mountains. Spain controlled this territory, though most of the settlers were French. The British, however, were entering the Dakotas to trade with Native people. Americans also eyed these western lands. In 1793, the Spanish formed the Missouri Company, based in St. Louis, to explore South Dakota. The Spanish were interested in trading with Native Americans and keeping the British out.

The next year, a Missouri Company **expedition** led by Jean Baptiste Truteau entered South Dakota. During this trip, Truteau built the first known European building in South Dakota, a small cabin near what is now Fort Randall. In 1800, a St. Louis trader named Régis Loisel built a larger fort south of present-day Pierre. Soon, however, the Spanish and French in Louisiana would find themselves residents of the United States.

LEWIS AND CLARK

In 1800, Spain secretly gave Louisiana to France, which had controlled that territory for most of the 18th century. Then in 1803, France sold Louisiana to the United States for $15 million, or about four cents an acre (0.4 ha). President Thomas Jefferson recruited Meriwether

Lewis and William Clark to lead an expedition through the new U.S. lands. Jefferson hoped to build good relations with Native American nations in the region and to find a water route to the Pacific.

The Lewis and Clark expedition began traveling up the Missouri River from St. Louis, Missouri, on May 14, 1804. They passed through South Dakota, and by winter reached today's North Dakota, where they met Sacagawea, a young Shoshone woman who became their leading interpreter. She was assisted by York, an enslaved African who had been Clark's companion since childhood. The members of the expedition gave Sacagawea and York the right to vote on expedition matters as a reward for their services and sacrifices.

The members of the expedition also met Arikaras, Yanktons, Yanktonais, and Lakotas. The expedition members got along well with Arikaras. But Lakotas along the Missouri near today's Pierre, South Dakota, would not let the expedition pass without paying a toll, and Lewis and Clark feared violence would break out. At first, Lewis and Clark refused to pay, but they finally offered a gift of tobacco.

The Louisiana Purchase nearly doubled the size of the United States. All or parts of 15 states were carved out of the Louisiana Territory, including South Dakota.

Louisiana Purchase

This map shows the area (in yellow) that made up the Louisiana Purchase and the present-day state of South Dakota (in orange).

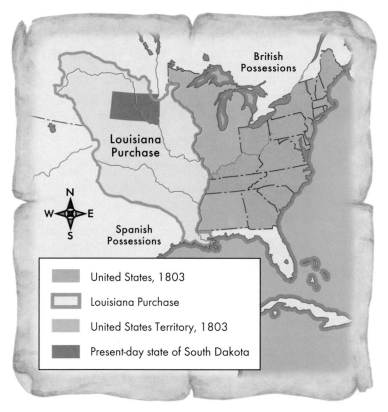

British Possessions

Louisiana Purchase

N
W—E
S

Spanish Possessions

United States, 1803

Louisiana Purchase

United States Territory, 1803

Present-day state of South Dakota

In South Dakota, Lewis and Clark captured a prairie dog and black-billed magpies and sent them back to President Jefferson in Washington, D.C.

WORD TO KNOW

naturalist *a person who studies natural history*

Sacagawea guiding the Lewis and Clark expedition

The expedition continued on and reached the Pacific Ocean in 1805. On the return trip to St. Louis, they once again passed through South Dakota's Lakota and Nakota villages. The expedition finally ended in September 1806.

TRADERS AND TRAPPERS

The Lewis and Clark expedition turned many American eyes toward the west. Foreigners were also interested in the wealth the Louisiana Territory held. In South Dakota, British, French, and Spanish traders joined Americans in the search for fur. Beaver was especially prized, as it was used in clothing in both the United States and Europe. Bison, deer, mink, and otter were also hunted for their skins and fur.

During the first decades of the 19th century, several large trading companies operated in South Dakota, the most important led by Pierre Chouteau, Jr. The companies traded metal tools, glass beads, guns, and other items to Native American trappers who brought their furs to the trading posts. Some trading posts were just small cabins, but Fort Pierre, which Chouteau built, was a major post, with palisade walls 15 feet (4.6 m) high and cannons defending it.

In 1831, Chouteau used a steamboat to bring goods to the region and take furs back to St. Louis. Steamboats could travel faster and carry more goods than boats that needed poles or oars.

Traders were not the only people who traveled through South Dakota. **Naturalist** John James Audubon visited the region to study birds and other wildlife, while artist George Catlin painted scenes of Sioux life. John C. Frémont led an expedition that explored lakes in eastern South Dakota.

Fort Pierre on the Upper Missouri River

SEE IT HERE!

SPIRIT MOUND

Historians are not sure about all the spots along the Missouri River where Lewis and Clark came ashore. But the explorers definitely reached South Dakota's Spirit Mound, 6 miles (10 km) north of Vermillion. Native people told the expedition that beings just 18 inches (46 cm) tall, with large heads, lived on the hill. Lewis, Clark, and several others walked four hours through intense summer heat to reach the hill. They didn't see any little people, but from the top they did see herds of bison. Today, Spirit Mound is a state park, and you can retrace the steps of the explorers to the top of the hill.

MANUEL LISA: SUCCESSFUL TRADER

When Lewis and Clark prepared for their mission, Manuel Lisa (1772–1820) helped supply them. Lisa, whose parents were Spanish, was born in New Orleans, Louisiana. He became a successful merchant in St. Louis, and in 1809, he and several other men formed the Missouri Fur Company. This company controlled the fur trade in South Dakota for several years, and Lisa made many trips to the region. He got along well with Native Americans, and he briefly worked for the U.S. government, handling Indian relations. More than any other person, he opened up trade along the Upper Missouri River.

? **Want to know more?** Visit www.factsfornow.scholastic.com and enter the keywords **South Dakota**.

Artist George Catlin

WORD TO KNOW

missionary *a person who tries to convert others to a religion*

In 1830, traders working along the Upper Missouri River sent 26,000 bison robes and 25,000 pounds (11,300 kilograms) of beaver fur to St. Louis.

Later, he would run for president. Priests and ministers also came to the region. A Belgian **missionary** named Pierre-Jean De Smet spent time trying to convert Nakota Sioux to Christianity.

LOSING THEIR LAND

Native Americans along the Missouri River and in the Great Plains received many goods by trading with Americans and Europeans. But at times, some fought with traders and explorers who entered their lands. In 1823, Arikaras attacked two boats traveling up the Missouri River, and the U.S. military sent troops to threaten the Arikaras. The U.S.

forces were joined by hundreds of Sioux, the Arikaras' traditional enemies. The Arikara people escaped, but by the mid-1800s, they had moved north, out of South Dakota.

In 1825, the U.S. government signed peace treaties with various Sioux groups. In the next few decades, however, more Americans moved west onto the Great Plains or passed through on their way to California and Oregon. The U.S. government wanted to move Native peoples to reservations. This would open Indian land to settlement and hopefully keep the peace.

In 1851, Lakotas and other Plains Indians met with U.S. officials at Fort Laramie, Wyoming. They agreed not to attack settlers heading west and to leave certain areas, though they would not go to reservations. In return, the U.S. officials promised to give the Indians goods worth $50,000 every year.

Trouble near Fort Laramie, however, soon led to an increased military presence in South Dakota. In 1854, a Brulé Lakota man killed a cow belonging to white settlers. Troops rode in, violence broke out, and Brulés killed all the U.S. soldiers. The next year, the U.S. government bought Fort Pierre to use as a military base. The fort was in bad shape, so in 1856, Fort Randall was built on the west side of the Missouri River, near the present-day South Dakota–Nebraska border. When the fort was complete, about 500 soldiers could live there.

Picture Yourself . . .

at Fort Laramie

You are a Lakota, and for several years you have seen a stream of white settlers venture across your land. You and some of your people decide to go to Fort Laramie, Wyoming, to meet with U.S. representatives. When you arrive, you see a vast camp of tipis. Ten thousand Plains Indians have gathered for the talks. Before the meeting begins, you dance and eat. A ceremonial cannon shot greets you and the others at the start of the talks. You listen as Indian leaders and U.S. officials speak of the need for peaceful relations. You watch as the leaders pass around a calumet, a ceremonial pipe that is a sign of their desire for peace. The leaders sign the treaty, and you leave the meeting hoping that the promises of peaceful relations will last.

In 1858, Yankton Sioux signed a treaty with the U.S. government. The Yankton people believed that the flood of white settlers into South Dakota could not be stopped. They agreed to surrender more than 11 million acres (4.4 million ha) of land and move to a reservation in exchange for $1.6 million.

GROWING SETTLEMENTS

European explorers and Americans from other areas had long traded furs at South Dakota forts, but for many years no permanent European-American town was founded in the region. Then in 1856, settlers from Iowa and Minnesota created the town of Sioux Falls at a large waterfall along the Big Sioux River. The first settlers built a fort, and 17 men spent the winter there. In 1859, the town of Yankton grew up on lands that Yankton Sioux had sold to the United States.

By 1861, South Dakotans convinced the U.S. Congress to create the Dakota Territory. This was the first step toward becoming a state. The original Dakota Territory included what is now North Dakota and South Dakota, Montana, and part of Wyoming. Yankton was named the capital. Two years later, Montana and Wyoming split off from the Dakota Territory.

MINI-BIO

JOHN BLAIR SMITH TODD: VOICE FOR DAKOTA

In 1855, John Blair Smith Todd (1814–1872) came to South Dakota as a U.S. Army officer. When he left the military the next year, he began working as a trader at Fort Randall. With his business partners, Todd helped convince the Yankton Sioux to sell their land to the U.S. government. He then helped found the city of Yankton and pushed for the creation of the Dakota Territory. With Todd's help, Yankton became the first capital of Dakota, and Todd served as the territory's first member of the U.S. House of Representatives.

? Want to know more? Visit www.factsfornow.scholastic.com and enter the keywords **South Dakota**.

A homestead near Sioux Falls, mid-1880s

During this time, about 1,000 whites and a handful of African Americans lived in South Dakota. At first, only white residents of the territory were allowed to vote. Over the next several decades, the territory's population exploded, as settlers of various backgrounds came to the prairies and plains. By 1880, 400 African American pioneers lived in South Dakota. They wanted to vote as much as other settlers, and they demanded their rights.

Soon South Dakotans of all backgrounds were pushing for more of a voice. They wanted statehood.

READ ABOUT

Settlers claiming
land in what is now
South Dakota, 1890

1872

*Construction begins
on South Dakota's
first railroad tracks*

◄1874

*George Custer leads
a military expedition
that finds gold in the
Black Hills*

1876

*Lakotas fight to
defend their lands*

CHAPTER FOUR

GROWTH AND CHANGE

★

SOUTH DAKOTA HAD WIDE-OPEN SPACES, AND THE BLACK HILLS WERE FILLED WITH PRECIOUS NATURAL RESOURCES. Americans from the East and immigrants from around the world were all eager to call South Dakota home. They brought their old ideas with them as they created new towns in South Dakota.

1878–1887
Thousands of homesteaders claim land during the Dakota land boom

1889 ►
South Dakota becomes the 40th state

1890
U.S. troops kill about 350 Lakotas at the Wounded Knee Massacre

The crew of a Union vessel, the USS *Hunchback*, on the James River, 1864

During the 1870s, huge swarms of grasshoppers sometimes destroyed crops across South Dakota. In 1874, almost all the corn grown between Yankton and Sioux Falls was lost.

IMMIGRANTS ARRIVE

Most of the first white settlers in South Dakota came from New England, New York, and other parts of the Northeast. Most traced their family roots to Great Britain. These newcomers were called Yankees.

The growth of new towns went slowly. In 1862, Dakota Sioux in western Minnesota battled newcomers because the United States had failed to live up to its treaty agreements. South Dakota settlers feared they would also have to fight for the land. Some fled to Yankton, and others simply left the territory. The fear of Indian attack lasted for several years, keeping new families from entering the region. The Civil War, which began in 1861, also hindered settlement. Several million men fought in the war between Northern and Southern states, and many others got jobs making war supplies in the East, so few people moved westward during this period.

After the Civil War ended in 1865, European immigrants began joining Yankees in the Dakota Territory.

Norwegians were the first major group. In the decades to come, they were joined by Swedes and Danes. Czechs, Germans, and Russian Germans followed. Many of the new arrivals worked as farmers, raising wheat, corn, and other crops in the prairies east of the Missouri River. Fur trapping and trading were no longer profitable in South Dakota, because most of the beavers had been killed and there was little demand for other furs.

IRON AND GOLD

Steamboats remained a major source of transportation in the Dakotas until 1872. That year, construction began on the territory's first railroad tracks. Railways ran to Yankton and Vermillion, making it easier to transport people and

FAQ

Q8 WHO WERE THE RUSSIAN GERMANS?

A8 During the 18th century, large groups of Germans settled in Russia, where they continued to keep their own language and their own culture. Beginning in the 1870s, thousands of these Russian Germans migrated to the United States to escape unfair treatment and service in the Russian army. In South Dakota, many settled in Eureka.

Sally Campbell, an African American cook, traveled with George Custer's Seventh Cavalry in 1874. She was the first non-Indian woman to visit the Black Hills. She later settled in Galena, in western South Dakota.

These engineers surveyed the land and prepared it for railroad construction in the Black Hills, 1888.

MINI-BIO

SITTING BULL: DEFENDER OF NATIVE LANDS

Tatanka-Iyotanka (c. 1831–1890), a Hunkpapa Lakota leader and medicine man, is generally known by his English name, Sitting Bull. In the 1860s, Sitting Bull battled U.S. troops in the Dakotas several times. When miners rushed to the Black Hills to search for gold, Sitting Bull swore he and his forces would keep the Americans out. After the Battle of the Little Bighorn, U.S. troops chased Sitting Bull and other Lakotas across South Dakota. For a time, Sitting Bull lived in Canada to avoid going to a reservation. Finally, in 1881, his people were starving because so few bison remained, and he agreed to move to a South Dakota reservation. Sitting Bull's courage and leadership continue to inspire people to this day.

? Want to know more? Visit www.factsfornow.scholastic.com and enter the keywords **South Dakota**.

African American U.S. Army regiments known as the Buffalo Soldiers helped keep the peace in the 1860s and 1870s. They were often given poor equipment, shoddy rifles, and old horses. But a dozen Buffalo Soldiers earned Congressional Medals of Honor defending western communities.

goods. Over the decades, the railroad lines slowly moved westward across the territory. Towns along the lines tended to grow, and those far away from them died. In some cases, entire towns moved to be closer to the railroads.

The railroads helped bring new settlers to the state. So did the lure of gold. As early as the 1850s, U.S. soldiers exploring the Black Hills reported seeing gold. The discovery of gold in Montana in the 1860s stimulated interest in the Black Hills. In 1874, Lieutenant Colonel George Custer led an expedition into the Black Hills to search for gold. When Custer and his men found gold, word spread across the nation. A gold rush began the next year, and miners poured into the region.

The arrival of the miners threatened the Lakota Sioux who lived in and around the Black Hills. During the 1850s, Lakota leader Sitting Bull had warned U.S. soldiers not to build forts or roads in the area.

Under an 1868 treaty, the U.S. government recognized the Lakotas' ancestral lands in western South Dakota as a reservation. Lakotas did not want limits placed on where they could live or hunt on their land. The 1868 treaty said settlers could not go to the Black Hills, but white miners ignored it.

The town of Deadwood during the Black Hills gold rush, 1870s

In 1876, Sitting Bull, a Lakota man named Crazy Horse, and others led Lakotas and their allies in a war against the United States. At the Battle of the Little Bighorn in Montana, Indians killed Custer and about 200 of his men. Soon, however, U.S. troops rounded up Native Americans on the northern plains, and the Black Hills were opened for white mining and settlement.

Deadwood and Lead (pronounced "leed") became the major towns in the Black Hills. They attracted miners, cowhands, and merchants who sold supplies. The miners were people from many backgrounds, including African Americans and Chinese. Deadwood became one of the

The Homestake Gold Mine in the Black Hills was the largest deposit of gold ever found in North America. It continued to produce gold until 2002.

MINI-BIO

FEE LEE WONG: SUCCESSFUL MERCHANT

Around 1870, Fee Lee Wong (1846–1921) left his homeland in China for the United States. Wong worked as a cook in the Black Hills. When robbers attacked the miners, Wong stood with them and helped fight. The miners rewarded his bravery by granting him the rights to two mines. Wong sold one and used the money to open a store in Deadwood's Chinatown, where most Chinese immigrants lived. In time, he bought several buildings and became one of the town's most successful merchants. His main building in Deadwood, called the Wing Tsue, survived until 2005. Archaeologists plan to study the site to look for items once used by Chinese Americans in Deadwood.

Want to know more? Visit www.factsfornow.scholastic.com and enter the keywords **South Dakota**.

wildest towns in the West. It was filled with saloons where people gambled and sometimes got into gunfights. "Wild Bill" Hickok, a sheriff and gunman, was killed in a Deadwood bar. Martha Jane Cannary, a frontier scout, was better known as Calamity Jane. She and Hickok are buried next to each other in Deadwood.

The gold rush ended in the 1880s, but people continued to work in the Black Hills. Some people still mined gold, while others cut trees for timber or raised cattle, horses, and other livestock.

THE DAKOTA BOOM

In 1862, Congress had passed the Homestead Act. This law let people have 160 acres (65 ha) of public land for free if they lived on it for five years and improved it in some way. Farming was the most common form of improvement. Settlers could claim the land in just six months if they paid for it. The people who settled on the land were called homesteaders.

From 1878 to 1887, thousands came to South Dakota to claim land. Investors also claimed some of the land, hoping to sell it for a profit in the future. During that time, people filed claims for more than 24 million acres (9.7 million ha) of land. The homesteaders included Benjamin, Patrick, and Mary Blair, whose parents had once been enslaved. They started a community of African Americans in Sully County called the Blair Colony.

Families traveled by wagon or railroad to the land they claimed. They used heavy-duty plows to churn up the prairie and prepare it for planting. Families had to dig deep wells for water. For heat, they sometimes burned buffalo chips (dried manure) if they could not find wood. To heat pans for cooking, settlers twisted together clumps of prairie grass and burned it. Children helped on the family farm, and some attended school in a private home. As towns grew, schools were built.

When families traveled west, they often packed all their belongings in covered wagons for the journey.

Picture Yourself . .

Living in a Sod House

You just moved to the South Dakota prairie from the East. Finally, your family has its own land to farm. The first thing you need to do when you arrive in South Dakota is build a house, but there are few trees around. Instead, you and your parents build a **sod** house. You dig up thick slices of the prairie—the tangle of prairie grass roots holds the soil together—and cut it into bricks. You stack the bricks to create a small house. Inside the house is a hard dirt floor. Dirt occasionally falls from the sod roof, and water sometimes streams in when it rains. Your sod house is cramped, so you don't spend much time inside it. But on the bright side, it is cool in the summer and warm in the winter. It won't catch fire, like a wooden house might. And you can grow flowers on your roof!

WORD TO KNOW

sod *soil thickly packed together with grass and roots*

A sod house in Newell

Over time, agriculture became more mechanized. Farmers began using steam-powered machines that could pull plows or cut crops. The machines were expensive, and most farmers still relied on animal power for their work. But mechanized farming slowly spread across South Dakota.

THE DAWES ACT

In 1887, the federal government passed the Dawes Act to encourage Native Americans to become farmers. The act split up reservation land owned by Native American nations and distributed it to individual Native Americans. If the individuals could not prove that they were farming

South Dakota: From Territory to Statehood

(1861–1889)

This map shows the original South Dakota territory and the area (in yellow) that became the state of South Dakota.

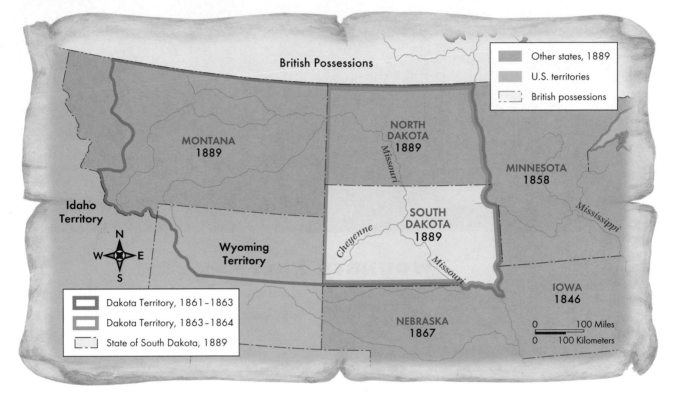

British Possessions

	Other states, 1889
	U.S. territories
	British possessions

MONTANA 1889

NORTH DAKOTA 1889

Missouri

MINNESOTA 1858

Idaho Territory

SOUTH DAKOTA 1889

Cheyenne

Mississippi

N
W · E
S

Wyoming Territory

Missouri

IOWA 1846

	Dakota Territory, 1861–1863
	Dakota Territory, 1863–1864
	State of South Dakota, 1889

NEBRASKA 1867

| 0 | 100 Miles |
| 0 | 100 Kilometers |

the land successfully, it was returned to the U.S. government. As a result, Native Americans lost millions of acres within a few years.

STATEHOOD

In 1880, fewer than 100,000 people lived in South Dakota. That number would almost triple in 10 years. Dakotans began pushing to divide the Dakota Territory into two states. In 1889, Congress granted their wishes, making South Dakota the 40th state. Its new capital was Pierre.

South Dakota entered the Union as a "dry" state, meaning buying and selling alcohol was illegal. That law stood until 1896.

A scene from the Wounded Knee Massacre, 1890

WOUNDED KNEE

In 1890, a new religion reached Indians in South Dakota. Followers of the Ghost Dance religion believed that special dances and prayers would help Native American nations regain their lands and way of life. The U.S. government believed the spread of the Ghost Dance was dangerous.

The government feared that the great Lakota leader Sitting Bull would practice the religion, encouraging other Sioux to accept it. Lakota police hired by the U.S. government came to the Standing Rock Reservation to arrest Sitting Bull, but instead they killed him. The Ghost Dancers fled, and some ended up near Wounded Knee Creek on the Pine Ridge Reservation in southwestern South Dakota. U.S. troops tracked them there. On December 29, 1890, the troops opened fire on the camp of Indian families. About 350 Lakotas were killed at the Wounded Knee Massacre. The Ghost Dance religion died as well.

POLITICAL CHANGES

By the 1890s, railroads were spreading across South Dakota. Farmers in the state began to fear that growth, because companies that owned the railroads controlled the economy. Farmers thought that these companies charged too much to carry grain to mills. South Dakota farmers struggled with bad weather, but banks expected them to pay back loans whether they could afford to or not. Some farming families formed the Populist Party to fight for their interests. In the late 1890s, Populists dominated the state government. They changed the state **constitution** so voters could propose laws,

WORD TO KNOW

constitution *a written document that contains all the governing principles of a state or country*

The Corn Palace in Mitchell

MAMIE SHIELDS PYLE: FIGHTER FOR WOMEN'S RIGHTS

Born in New Jersey, Mamie Shields Pyle (1866–1949) settled in Huron, South Dakota, in 1889. Pyle took a strong interest in politics and demanded suffrage, or the right to vote, for women. During the 1910s, she was president of the South Dakota State Suffrage Association. With her leadership, South Dakota women won the right to vote in 1918—two years before all U.S. women won that right. Toward the end of her life, Pyle was named the state's Mother of the Year. This honor came after she proudly saw her daughter Gladys become South Dakota's first female lawmaker.

? Want to know more? Visit www.factsfor now.scholastic.com and enter the keywords **South Dakota**.

Governor Peter Norbeck was in office from 1917 to 1921.

Q8 WHAT WAS PROGRESSIVISM?

A8 Progressivism was a movement to improve lives for workers, farmers, women, and children. Progressives wanted to give the average American more control in politics and end the influence of big business.

a process called the initiative. Voters could also reject or accept certain laws passed by the legislature, a process called the referendum.

The Populists were not able to stop the overwhelming power of huge corporations in South Dakota's politics and economy. But their efforts led to many reforms and paved the way for a new effort led by the progressives. A progressive Republican named Peter Norbeck served as governor from 1917 to 1921. Under Norbeck, the state government offered low-interest loans to farmers. It also provided insurance for crops damaged by hail and paid money to workers injured on the job. The progressive movement remained strong in South Dakota for several decades.

WORLD WAR I AND AFTER

In 1914, fighting broke out among several European nations, marking the start of World War I. The United States entered the war in 1917, and South Dakotans did their part to help. About 32,000 of them joined the military. Farmers increased production, because the U.S. government was sending food to its allies. The demand for crops led to more money for farmers.

When the war ended in 1918, farmers were still enjoying high prices for their crops. But nature and world events would conspire to create many challenges in the coming decades.

A South Dakota farmer plows a beet field, early 1900s

58

READ ABOUT

A view of Aberdeen, early 1900s

1930–1936

Severe drought strikes South Dakota

1933

New Deal programs begin helping South Dakotans during the Great Depression

▲ 1941–1945

Thousands of South Dakotans, including Sioux code talkers, fight in World War II

CHAPTER FIVE

MORE MODERN TIMES

★

FOR MOST OF THE NATION, THE EARLY 1920s WERE A PROSPEROUS TIME. But that was not the case for South Dakota farmers. The demand for their crops fell, so prices fell. Some farmers lost their land because they couldn't pay their debts, and banks began to close. Still, some South Dakotans bought radios and cars. And the government built more paved roads, which attracted tourists to the state.

1946
Work begins on four dams across the Missouri River

1979
Lakotas are awarded more than $100 million for the loss of their lands in the Black Hills but refuse to take it

▲2012
South Dakota leads the nation in energy generated by wind power

SEE IT HERE!

MOUNT RUSHMORE

In 1923, South Dakota historian Doane Robinson promoted the idea of carving a giant sculpture into the rocks of the Black Hills to attract more tourists to the area. U.S. senator Peter Norbeck pressed for federal support. Robinson contacted artist Gutzon Borglum, who chose Mount Rushmore as the site. From 1927 to 1941, workers cut giant heads of four American presidents—George Washington, Thomas Jefferson, Theodore Roosevelt, and Abraham Lincoln—into the side of the mountain. Today, more than 2.5 million people visit Mount Rushmore each year, making it South Dakota's most popular tourist attraction.

Mount Rushmore was under construction from 1927 to 1941.

HARD TIMES

South Dakota's farm problems worsened after 1929, when the entire country entered the Great Depression, the worst economic crisis in U.S. history. Across the country, millions of people lost their jobs and sometimes their homes. Thousands of banks closed, wiping out people's savings. Many South Dakota farmers lost their land. Those who continued to farm faced severe drought in the 1930s

The first speed limit in Sioux Falls was enacted in 1903. Cars could not go faster than 7 miles per hour (11 kph) on straight roads and 4 mph (6 kph) around corners.

and watched as the fertile topsoil blew away in "black blizzards."

In 1933, President Franklin D. Roosevelt began a series of programs called the New Deal, which were intended to relieve suffering from lack of work and income during the Great Depression. Some New Deal programs put people to work building libraries or improving parks. Others helped farmers. Under one program, farmers in South Dakota and elsewhere received money if they did not grow certain crops. Reducing the supply caused prices to rise. The government money helped farmers pay their debts, and they could receive government loans at low interest rates. Farmers also received money if they grew crops such as soybeans, which were good for the soil.

BLACK BLIZZARDS

One of the worst droughts in South Dakota history began in 1930. By 1933, strong winds sometimes picked up the dry soil and carried it for miles. The clouds of dirt blackened the skies in what were called black blizzards. The blowing dirt buried cars and tractors. One newspaper reported, "The roofs of sheds stuck out through drifts deeper than a man is tall." Rainfall finally returned to normal in 1936, ending the drought.

These laborers for the Works Progress Administration, a New Deal program, help build a bridge near Pierre.

MEDICAL PIONEER

The daughter of a doctor, Abbie Jarvis (1854–1931) waited a long time before pursuing her own medical career. She and her husband moved to South Dakota in 1880, eventually settling in Faulkton. When she was in her late 30s, Jarvis went to medical school. She graduated in 1898, becoming South Dakota's first female doctor. She made house calls to remote farms, often delivering babies. She safely brought more than 600 children into the world, and they were sometimes called Jarvis babies. She continued her medical practice through the 1920s, almost until the time of her death.

WORLD WAR II

The New Deal programs helped millions of Americans, but they did not end the Great Depression. Only the coming of World War II ended the economic problems. War broke out in Europe in September 1939, as Great Britain, France, and other countries battled German forces. U.S. factories were soon bustling with activity, as the country supplied its European allies. Then on December 7, 1941, Japan launched a surprise attack on the U.S. naval base in Pearl Harbor, Hawai'i. The United States declared war on Japan, Germany, and Italy.

Once again, thousands of South Dakotans volunteered to fight. Many Sioux soldiers won praise for their battle-

Troops of the 34th Infantry—including soldiers from Minnesota, North Dakota, and South Dakota—in Italy, 1943

Native American code talkers assigned to a marine unit during World War II

MINI-BIO

JOE FOSS: WAR HERO AND MORE

Joe Foss (1915–2003) was just 11 when he went to an air show in Sioux Falls. After that, he knew he wanted to fly. He already had his pilot's license when World War II began, and soon he was flying fighter planes for the U.S. Marines. Foss became a national hero after shooting down 26 planes and earning the Congressional Medal of Honor. After the war, he entered politics, eventually serving as South Dakota's governor for four years. In 1959, he became president of the American Football League, which later became part of the National Football League.

❓ **Want to know more?** Visit www.factsfor now.scholastic.com and enter the keywords **South Dakota**.

field skills, while others worked as "code talkers," sending and receiving messages in codes spoken in their native languages. These codes were virtually impossible to break since almost no one except Native Americans could speak the languages on which they were based. Eleven Sioux from South Dakota served as code talkers during the war.

Many South Dakotans moved to other states to take jobs in factories making military equipment. The farmers who remained in South Dakota stepped up their crop production to feed soldiers fighting around the world. Their flax was turned into linen, which was used to make uniforms. And South Dakota soybeans were turned into oil used in cooking.

Thousands of Americans came to South Dakota to train or work at military bases. The Army Air Corps established a training base for radio operators in Sioux Falls. Both Pierre and Rapid City also had army air bases. And in the Black Hills, near Edgemont, the government stored ammunition.

POSTWAR CHANGES

After the war ended in 1945, many South Dakotans continued to work at or near military bases. But the daily activities of most people in the state revolved around farming. They either raised crops and livestock, transported them, or provided services and equipment to farmers. Still, life was changing in South Dakota. Electricity, which had once been limited to towns, was reaching more farms, and car ownership continued to grow. The state had lost population in the 1930s, but the numbers were inching

The busy streets of Aberdeen, 1960s

back up. Just over 650,000 people lived there in 1950, about 10,000 more than in 1940.

Most of the growth occurred in larger towns and cities. In rural areas, young people left farms to find jobs in towns and cities. The drain of rural residents continued when two new interstate highways appeared in the early 1960s. Interstate 90 cut the state in half from east to west. The other, Interstate 29, traveled from north to south in the eastern part of the state. Towns far from the highway began to die—just as others had when the railroad tracks bypassed them in the 1880s.

Between 1946 and 1966, one of the biggest projects in the state was the construction of four dams across the Missouri River. The dams created huge **reservoirs**, which covered about 500,000 acres (202,000 ha) of land, including some valuable farmland. The dams were built to help control floods and provide **irrigation** for farmland. They also created electricity, and the new lakes became popular recreation areas.

LAKOTA STRUGGLES

Through the 20th century, Sioux families often had trouble adjusting to life on reservations. Lakotas in particular struggled to become farmers and ranchers as the government wanted. Some rented their land to white farmers, while other Sioux left the reservations to find jobs out of state.

In 1934, the U.S. Commissioner of Indian Affairs issued an order that gave all Native Americans greater freedom to follow their traditional culture. Congress passed a law to allow them more freedom to run their own affairs. Still, for the Sioux of South Dakota, life remained difficult.

By the late 1960s, some Sioux wanted to take action. Russell Means, an Oglala Lakota, became one of the leaders of the American Indian Movement (AIM). AIM wanted

WORDS TO KNOW

reservoirs *artificial lakes or tanks for storing water*

irrigation *watering land by artificial means to promote plant growth*

WOW

In 1980, the U.S. Supreme Court ruled that the Lakota people should receive more than $100 million to pay for their earlier loss of the Black Hills. Lakotas refused the money, because they still wanted the land.

MINI-BIO

RUSSELL MEANS: LAKOTA ACTIVIST

Russell Means (1939–2012) was born to a Yankton mother and Oglala father on the Pine Ridge Indian Reservation. In 1969, he joined the American Indian Movement (AIM). Means wanted the U.S. government to return Indian lands and treat Native Americans fairly. He joined protests at Mount Rushmore and Plymouth Rock before going to Wounded Knee in 1973. Until his death, Means continued to speak out for Native American rights.

? **Want to know more?** Visit www.factsfor now.scholastic.com and enter the keywords **South Dakota**.

the U.S. government to help end poverty and legal inequality for all Native Americans. In 1973, Means and other Sioux went to Wounded Knee to protest conditions on the reservations. A gun battle broke out between some of the Indians and U.S. officials, and two Indians died. Although AIM was criticized for some its tactics, the group's action led the U.S. government to give Native Americans more self-rule and protection for their traditional ways.

Russell Means, Dennis Banks, and Carter Camp (left to right) make a peace agreement with Methodist bishop James Armstrong at Wounded Knee, 1970s.

Grain being harvested on a South Dakota farm

RECENT TIMES

During the late 1970s and early 1980s, South Dakota farmers faced new economic problems. Farmers were too successful: they grew so much grain that prices fell. Farmers still had debts to pay, with no money to pay them. Over time, more small farmers went out of business. Farmers with more land were usually able to survive. Many even grew as they took over failing small farms.

New industries came to South Dakota in the 1980s. Governor Bill Janklow pushed for changes in state banking laws. This attracted several large banks to Sioux Falls. They ran their credit card services in the city, where the population grew by 23 percent in the 1990s. Sioux Falls also became the center for health care in the state. The arrival of new companies drew new immigrants to South Dakota. In addition, tourism thrived, and the state worked

A ranger takes a group on a hike through Badlands National Park.

to preserve existing industries. When a major railroad line that ran through South Dakota went out of business, the state bought the railroad. It rented the line to another railroad company, which saved thousands of jobs in South Dakota and kept goods flowing throughout the state.

In the 21st century, the United States began looking for new sources of energy so it would not have to rely so heavily on oil. Fuel could be made from corn, soybeans, and other crops, and South Dakota farmers saw prices for these goods rise as demand increased.

New Energy Sources

About 300 million bushels of corn grown in South Dakota each year are used to make ethanol, a type of fuel. One bushel of corn produces 2.8 gallons (10.6 liters) of ethanol. That's a lot of environmentally friendly fuel for cars and other motor-driven machines! However, not everyone thinks that corn should be turned into fuel.

PRO

Supporters argue that ethanol will make the United States less dependent on foreign sources of energy, such as oil. "Vehicles that can use . . . ethanol could be the answer to fuel shortages and large spikes in pump prices," said Mike Johnson, a spokesperson for the Renewable Fuels Association.

CON

Some people believe that using corn to make ethanol reduces the world's food supply. "Four of every ten ears of corn grown in America—the source of 40 percent of the world's production—are shunted into ethanol, a gasoline substitute that [barely] nicks our energy problem," said Steven Rattner, a lead adviser to the Presidential Task Force on the Auto Industry in 2009. "What is more, making corn ethanol consumes vast quantities of water and increases smog."

Today, many South Dakotans believe that the state's natural beauty, low taxes, and a hardworking labor force make it well prepared to face the challenges of the future.

READ ABOUT

Visitors to the Central States Fair in Rapid City enjoy a thrill ride.

CHAPTER SIX

PEPLE

★

M ANY OF THE TOWNS ON SOUTH DAKOTA'S PRAIRIES AND PLAINS ARE GROWING. The population rise is fueled by new arrivals from Spanish-speaking countries, as well as Africa and Asia. But some parts of the state are still sparsely populated. Take a drive and you might see just one or two homes for miles and miles. South Dakota is still a land of wide-open spaces.

South Dakota Population Growth

This chart shows South Dakota's population changes between 1860 and 2010.

Source: U.S. Census Bureau, 2010 census

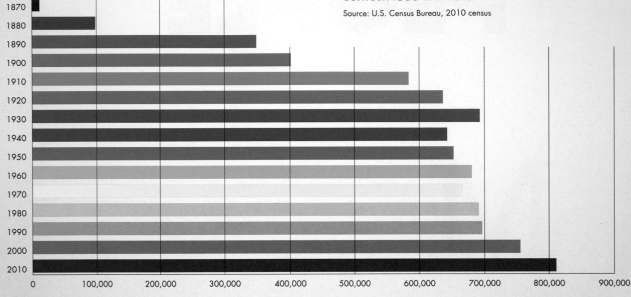

AT HOME IN SOUTH DAKOTA

Just over 800,000 people live in South Dakota's 77,116 square miles (199,730 sq km). That gives the state one of the lowest population densities in the country, with just under 11 people for every square mile (4 per sq km). The largest population centers are found at either end of the state near the two major cities, Sioux Falls and Rapid City.

ONE STATE, DIFFERENT BACKGROUNDS

Since the 19th century, most South Dakotans have traced their roots to either Sioux or European nations. Today, Native Americans make up about 9 percent of the population, one of the highest percentages among the states.

Big City Life

This list shows the population of South Dakota's biggest cities.

City	Population
Sioux Falls	153,888
Rapid City	67,956
Aberdeen	26,091
Brookings	22,056
Watertown	21,482

Source: U.S. Census Bureau, 2010 census

The state's white population includes people from the British Isles, **Scandinavia**, and Germany. In 2012, about 43 percent of South Dakotans said they had family ties to Germany, making German Americans the largest ethnic group. They were followed by Norwegians with 15 percent and Irish with 11 percent.

In recent years, the Hispanic population of South Dakota has seen marked growth. From 2005 to 2010, the number of Hispanics grew from about 14,000 to more than 22,000. Many of the new arrivals came from Mexico and Central America. Many took jobs working in meat-processing plants in the southeastern part of the state. The number of South Dakotans of Asian descent is small but growing, and most settle in the more urban areas of

The Oglala Lakota, with almost 47,000 members, is the largest tribe in South Dakota.

WORD TO KNOW

Scandinavia *a region of northern Europe made up of Sweden, Norway, Denmark, Finland, and Iceland*

A couple captures the view at Badlands National Park.

Q: WHO ARE THE HUTTERITES?

A: The Hutterites are a small Protestant group who trace their roots to Russian German settlers of South Dakota. The Hutterites own all their property as a group and live in communities called colonies. They oppose war and live simple lives, often making their own clothing and furniture. South Dakota's Hutterites are excellent farmers, raising most of the turkeys and hogs produced in the state.

the eastern part of the state. In the past, few African Americans settled in the state, and while their numbers are slowly growing today, they remain a tiny part of the population. Some newcomers arrive from African nations such as Sudan, Ethiopia, Somali, and Liberia.

CITY LIFE, RURAL LIFE

Once, most South Dakotans lived a rural life in small towns. Since 1990, the state's population has become slightly more urban than rural. And modern technology such as satellites and the Internet connect remote parts of South Dakota to the larger world.

Sioux Falls is the major urban center in the state. Suburbs are growing around the city as businesses and workers move to the area.

Most of South Dakota is still a land of small towns. The state has strong, closely knit communities, where people help each other during bad times and come together to celebrate the good. Still, many young South Dakotans think their small hometowns don't provide enough entertainment or good jobs. They often leave the towns for larger cities both in and out of South Dakota.

People QuickFacts

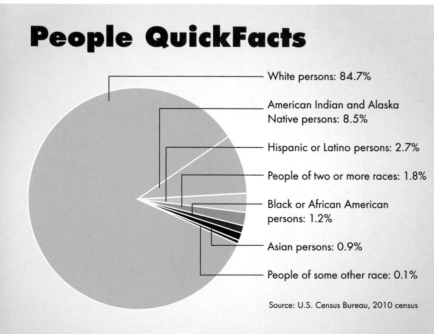

White persons: 84.7%

American Indian and Alaska Native persons: 8.5%

Hispanic or Latino persons: 2.7%

People of two or more races: 1.8%

Black or African American persons: 1.2%

Asian persons: 0.9%

People of some other race: 0.1%

Source: U.S. Census Bureau, 2010 census

Where South Dakotans Live

The colors on this map indicate population density throughout the state. The darker the color, the more people live there.

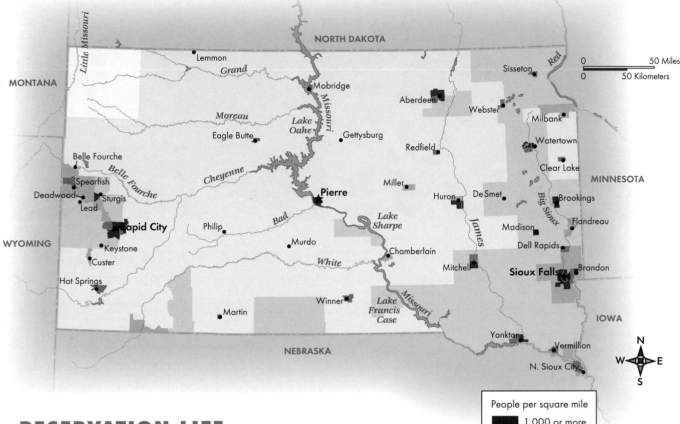

People per square mile

■	1,000 or more
■	200 to 1,000
■	88 to 200
■	20 to 88
■	5 to 20
■	1 to 5
□	1 or fewer

RESERVATION LIFE

South Dakota's nine Indian reservations are home to just over 100,000 people. On the reservations, many Sioux blend their traditional spiritual beliefs with modern ways of life. However, reservation life can be difficult. Unemployment is high. Rates of diseases such as diabetes, cancer, and heart disease are higher than the U.S. national averages. Many residents must travel long distances for health care services. The school dropout rate is also high, and most reservation schools receive the lowest amount of funding by the U.S. government in the country.

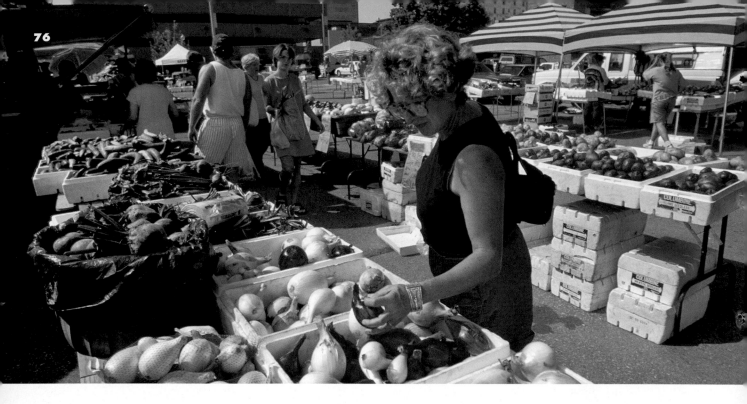

A farmers' market in Sioux Falls

HOW TO TALK LIKE A SOUTH DAKOTAN

When you go to a grocery store, your purchases will likely be put in a "sack" rather than a "bag." And when you visit the state capital, talk like a native and call it "Peer"—South Dakotans don't use the French pronunciation of Pierre (pee-AIR). Say "East River" and "West River" to describe the eastern and western halves of the state, and folks might think you're a local. And if you meet some Dakota Sioux, you can greet them in their native language by saying *Hau koda*, or "Welcome, friend!"

HOW TO EAT LIKE A SOUTH DAKOTAN

You'd expect a farm state to produce lots of hearty meals, and South Dakota doesn't let you down. Beef is often on the menu, but so are wild animals from the state's forests and fish from the state's streams. Grains such as wheat and corn are used in many dishes. And the different settlers of the state, from Sioux to Germans, have added their favorite foods to the state's meals.

MENU

WHAT'S ON THE MENU IN SOUTH DAKOTA?

★ ★ ★

Kuchen

Buffalo burger

Buffalo Burgers

Bison (buffalo) were once almost extinct. Now South Dakota ranchers raise the shaggy beasts for their meat. Bison is low in fat compared to beef. Besides burgers, bison meat is also used for steaks and sausages.

Wasna/Pemmican

When bison and other game were scarce on the plains, the Sioux turned to a food that could last for years. They called it *wasna* (wah-SHNA), though today it's better known as pemmican. Wasna is packed with protein and other things your body needs. Traditional wasna was made with dried bison meat, chokecherries (a type of fruit), and animal fat.

Pheasant

Hunters stalk these game birds over two-thirds of the state, and they've come up with lots of ways to prepare them. Pheasant meat is used in soups and casseroles, while some folks prefer it simply roasted.

TRY THIS RECIPE
Kuchen

The Russian Germans of South Dakota perfected this sweet treat, which is the German word for "cake." People make many different types of kuchen, which can look like a coffee cake or a pie. Most recipes include a custard filling, and some kuchen are filled with fruit. Have an adult nearby to help you make this apple kuchen.

Batter Ingredients:
1 cup milk
2 eggs
⅔ cup flour
2 teaspoons sugar
½ teaspoon grated lemon zest
½ teaspoon salt
2 tablespoons butter

Filling Ingredients:
2 cups thickly sliced apples
2 tablespoons butter
3 tablespoons sugar
½ teaspoon cinnamon

Instructions:
1. Preheat the oven to 400°F.
2. Mix the milk, eggs, flour, sugar, salt, and lemon zest together in a bowl to make the batter.
3. Melt the butter in a skillet. Put the melted butter in a 9-inch pie plate and then pour the batter into the pie plate.
4. Bake the kuchen for 30 to 35 minutes, until it is golden brown.
5. While the kuchen is baking, peel and slice the apples.
6. Melt the butter in a skillet, and then cook the apples, sugar, and cinnamon in the butter over medium heat until the apples are tender.
7. After removing the kuchen from the oven, pour the apple filling in its center, and serve immediately.

Some South Dakota public schools hold classes just four days per week. Cutting out a day helps towns save money. The students make up the time by having longer hours on each of the four days.

EDUCATION

On school days, South Dakota's students in grades K–12 head out to either public or private schools. The state has just over 800 schools, including many on reservations. At Indian schools, students learn their native language along with the same subjects taught in other schools.

The state's largest public university is South Dakota State University in Brookings, which has strong programs in agriculture and nursing. The University of South Dakota in Vermillion is home to the state's only medical school and law school.

A WAY WITH WORDS

Many South Dakotans have written novels that delve into their experiences with the state's lonely prairies and rugged mountains. Hamlin Garland didn't spend much time in South Dakota, but his book *Main-Travelled Roads* described pioneer life in the state. O. E. Rolvaag, a Norwegian immigrant, worked and studied in South Dakota and wrote three novels that illustrate the pioneer experience. During World War II, Borghild Dahl wrote books about her own blindness and immigrant life.

More recently, Lakota writer Virginia Driving Hawk Sneve has entertained and educated both children and adults with her work. Her children's books include *When Thunders Spoke* and *Jimmy Yellow*

MINI-BIO

LAURA INGALLS WILDER: PIONEER WRITER

Laura Ingalls Wilder (1867–1957) spent part of her childhood in a house near De Smet, South Dakota. She watched the prairie change and towns grow, and later wrote a series of nine children's books about her pioneer childhood, known as the Little House series. Her books have sold tens of millions of copies around the world and sparked the hit TV show *Little House on the Prairie*. By telling her family's stories, Wilder also told the history of South Dakota pioneer life.

Want to know more? Visit www.factsfor now.scholastic.com and enter the keywords **South Dakota**.

Hawk. Paul Goble, who lives in Rapid City, has also written and illustrated many children's books that often deal with Native American life.

VISUAL ARTS

Visual art has a long history in South Dakota. Thousands of years ago, Native people carved images into rocks, often showing human or animal figures. Several hundred years ago, Sioux artists recorded their people's history by drawing images on dried animal skins. Many modern Sioux artists were influenced by Oscar Howe, a Yanktonai Nakota who blended traditional Native American forms with the ideas of modern art. Other artists in South Dakota include Terry Redlin, who was inspired by South Dakota communities and wildlife, and Harvey Dunn, who illustrated scenes of American life for many magazines.

Artist Terry Redlin

MINI-BIO

OSCAR HOWE: PAINTER

Oscar Howe (1915–1983) was the great-grandson of two Yanktonai Nakota chiefs. Growing up on the Crow Creek Reservation, he learned about Sioux history and culture. He wanted to draw the stories he heard, but his father did not want him to become an artist and took away his pencils. Oscar then found some charcoal and used that to draw. As an adult, Howe blended traditional Indian techniques with the skills he learned in art school. His paintings often featured geometric shapes, such as triangles, lines, and arcs. He continues to influence South Dakota artists today.

? **Want to know more?** Visit www.factsfor now.scholastic.com and enter the keywords **South Dakota**.

MINI-BIO

OSCAR MICHEAUX: HOMESTEADER AND FILMMAKER

In 1904, near the Rosebud Reservation, Oscar Micheaux (1884–1951) bought land another farmer had given up. He encouraged other African Americans to join him in South Dakota, and he wrote several books about his experience there. In 1919, Micheaux turned one of those books into a film called *The Homesteader*, the first full-length film made by an African American. He went on to create about 40 films. These movies starred black actors and were made for African American audiences. Though many of Micheaux's works have been lost, he was central in putting the African American experience on film.

? **Want to know more?** Visit www.factsfornow.scholastic.com and enter the keywords **South Dakota**.

A Lakota leader and medicine man is the subject of one of the largest sculptures in the state. In the Badlands, a statue of Crazy Horse is slowly being carved into a mountain. Artist Korczak Ziolkowski began the sculpture in 1948.

THE WORLD OF SPORTS

South Dakota doesn't have any major professional sports teams, but it does field teams in several minor leagues. Sioux Falls has a baseball team, the Canaries; a

The work on this Crazy Horse sculpture in the Badlands began in 1948.

MINI-BIO

BILLY MILLS: OLYMPIC SPEEDSTER

Billy Mills (1938—) grew up in poverty on the Pine Ridge Indian Reservation for Oglala Lakota people. By the time he was 12 years old, both of his parents had died. To ease his loss, Mills took up running. After graduating from the University of Kansas, he enlisted in the marines. But Mills still loved to run, and he qualified for the 1964 Summer Olympics. In the 10,000-meter race, Mills sped to victory, winning a gold medal—and becoming the first American to win the event.

? **Want to know more?** Visit www.factsfor now.scholastic.com and enter the keywords **South Dakota**.

A cowboy rides a bucking bronco in a rodeo in Belle Fourche.

hockey team, the Stampede; and a basketball team, the Skyforce. Many sports fans in the state cheer on teams from the University of South Dakota and South Dakota State University.

One of the top sports in South Dakota traces its roots to ranching on the frontier. Rodeos feature cowboys and cowgirls riding horses, roping cattle, and racing horses around barrels. One of rodeo's greatest stars, Casey Tibbs, grew up on the frontier west of Fort Pierre. More recently, Jesse Bail from Spearfish has been a professional rodeo star. Today, rodeo is South Dakota's official state sport.

READ ABOUT

An inside look at the dome of the South Dakota capitol

CHAPTER SEVEN

GOVERNMENT

★

I N SOUTH DAKOTA, PROJECT CITIZEN HELPS KIDS START LEARNING ABOUT GOVERNMENT EARLY. With the project, students study important issues and then present their views to government officials. Students in a class in Pollock studied the Missouri River reservoirs and noticed that water levels were low. The students believed that using the water for drinking should be a main priority, and they took their findings to state lawmakers. The students learned firsthand about the role all citizens can play in running a government.

84

The state capitol in Pierre

WORD TO KNOW

petition *a formal written request signed by a group of voters*

In 1898, South Dakota became the first state to allow voters to have their say through the initiative and referendum processes.

THE CENTER OF STATE GOVERNMENT

The center of government is in Pierre, the state capital. The state legislature, the supreme court, and the governor's office are all located here.

The details of South Dakota's government are spelled out in the state constitution. The first version of this document was written in 1889, and amendments have been added to it over the years. Voters in South Dakota can propose new amendments or new laws in a process called an initiative. If enough people sign a **petition**, the proposed law is placed on the ballot during an election.

Capital City

This map shows places of interest in Pierre, South Dakota's capital city.

South Dakota Discovery Center & Aquarium

South Dakota State Historical Society

PIERRE

Missouri River

South Dakota State Capitol

Capitol Facts

Here are some fascinating facts about South Dakota's state capitol.

Size: 292 feet (89 m) long, 190 feet (58 m) wide, 161 feet (49 m) high, with an area of more than 114,000 square feet (10,591 sq m)

Year completed: 1915; restoration done from 1975 to 1989

Cost of original building: Just under $1 million

SEE IT HERE!

THE CAPITOL

South Dakota's capitol is topped with an impressive copper dome, and visitors can explore the building every day of the year. Inside the capitol is a doll collection showing small versions of gowns worn by governors' wives. The building also has four sculptures called *Wisdom, Vision, Courage*, and *Integrity*, and paintings of goddesses from Greek mythology. On the capitol grounds are several more statues and memorials.

If more people vote for the proposed law than against it, the law is put into effect. South Dakotans can also vote to prevent a law passed by the legislature from taking effect, in a process called a referendum. Voters say yes or no to keeping the law. A recall allows citizens to remove a public official before the end of his or her term of office.

LEGISLATIVE BRANCH

South Dakota's legislature includes the house of representatives and the senate. Both the house and the senate must approve a bill before it is sent to the governor to be signed into law.

South Dakota State Government

EXECUTIVE BRANCH
Carries out state laws

| Governor | Lieutenant Governor | Attorney General | Secretary of State | Treasurer | Auditor | Commissioner of School and Public Lands |

JUDICIAL BRANCH
Enforces state laws

Supreme Court

Circuit Courts

Magistrate Courts

Department heads of:
Agriculture
Corrections
Education
Environment
Health
Housing
and many more

LEGISLATIVE BRANCH
Makes and passes state laws

Senate (35 members)

House of Representatives (70 members)

Representing South Dakota

This list shows the number of elected officials who represent South Dakota, both on the state and national levels.

OFFICE	NUMBER	LENGTH OF TERM
State senators	35	2 years
State representatives	70	2 years
U.S. senators	2	6 years
U.S. representatives	1	2 years
Presidential electors	3	—

EXECUTIVE BRANCH

The executive branch in South Dakota includes seven positions that are chosen by voters. The most important is governor. The governor must sign a bill for it to become law. He or she may also veto it to reject it. The state legislature can override a veto if two-thirds of the members in each house vote again for the bill. As leader of the executive branch, the governor chooses people to lead various executive departments. The senate must approve most of these choices. The governor proposes a budget for the state, but

Governor Dennis Daugaard signs a bill to reform South Dakota's criminal justice system in 2013.

state lawmakers have the final say on how much money is spent and where it goes. The governor can also rally lawmakers and citizens to support new ideas.

The lieutenant governor of South Dakota serves as president of the state senate but does not vote unless there is a tie. He or she also takes over if the governor leaves office. The secretary of state has duties such as running elections and registering voters. The attorney general makes sure the state's laws are enforced and

The South Dakota House of
Representatives gathers in 2013.

represents South Dakota in legal matters. The treasurer invests the state's money, while the state auditor makes sure people pay their taxes and that tax money is spent legally. The commissioner of schools and public lands watches over the money the state makes from the sale of land and its natural resources. These include oil, natural gas, and minerals. Most of the money earned from these resources goes to the state's schools.

JUDICIAL BRANCH

The most powerful court in the state is the supreme court. The governor appoints its five judges, called justices, who choose one of their own to serve as chief justice. Three years after justices are first named to the court, voters decide if they will remain on the court. Those who remain face new elections every eight years. The supreme court decides if rulings made in lower courts were legally correct. Supreme court justices also decide how the lower courts will be run, and they can give legal advice when a governor asks for it.

The circuit courts of South Dakota hear all cases involving crimes or disputes between citizens. Thirty-eight judges are elected to serve in seven circuits across the state. The chief justice of the state supreme court chooses a chief judge for each circuit. For less serious crimes and disputes, cases go to the magistrate courts.

MINI-BIO

DENNIS DAUGAARD: GOVERNOR

Dennis Daugaard (1953—) was raised on a farm near Garretson in the eastern part of South Dakota by parents who were both deaf. A graduate of the University of South Dakota, he entered politics in 1997 and was elected as a state senator, serving from 1997 to 2003. After serving two terms as lieutenant governor, he became governor in 2011. As governor, Daugaard has focused on creating jobs by bringing new businesses to the state.

? **Want to know more?** Visit www.factsfor now.scholastic.com and enter the keywords **South Dakota**.

GOVERNMENT CLOSER TO HOME

Like other states, South Dakota has lawmakers and executives who govern at the local level. South Dakota is divided into 66 counties, each with its own government. Voters elect county commissioners, who act as both the legislature and executive branch. Other elected positions include treasurer, auditor, sheriff, and state's attorney. Within each county are various cities, towns, and districts. Voters elect people to serve on boards that pass **ordinances** and collect taxes. Local and county governments build schools and libraries, hire police officers, maintain roads, and provide other essential public services.

WORD TO KNOW

ordinances *laws passed by local governments*

Members of the Oglala Sioux Nation perform traditional chants as former U.S. president Bill Clinton (rear center) looks on, 1999.

BEN REIFEL: LAWMAKER

Ben Reifel (1906–1990) journeyed from a South Dakota log cabin to the U.S. Capitol. He grew up on the Rosebud Reservation, the son of a Brulé Lakota mother and German American father. After college, he worked for the U.S. Bureau of Indian Affairs. He helped Native Americans in South Dakota set up new tribal governments. In 1960, Reifel entered politics and won a seat in the U.S. House of Representatives, making him the first Sioux to serve in Congress. He worked hard for all voters in his district, Sioux and non-Indian alike, and was reelected four times.

 Want to know more? Visit www.factsfornow.scholastic.com and enter the keywords **South Dakota**.

South Dakota Counties

This map shows the 66 counties in South Dakota. Pierre, the state capital, is indicated with a star.

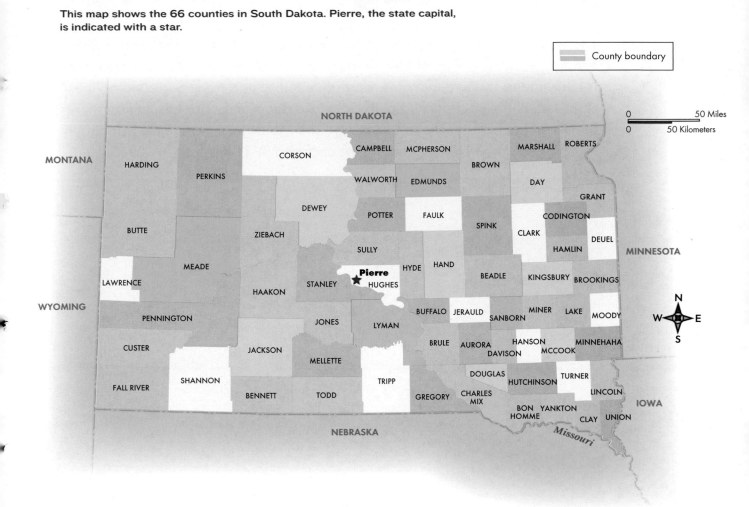

County boundary

0   50 Miles
0   50 Kilometers

NORTH DAKOTA

MONTANA

MINNESOTA

WYOMING

NEBRASKA

IOWA

HARDING
PERKINS
CORSON
CAMPBELL
MCPHERSON
MARSHALL
ROBERTS
WALWORTH
EDMUNDS
BROWN
DAY
GRANT
BUTTE
DEWEY
POTTER
FAULK
SPINK
CODINGTON
CLARK
HAMLIN
DEUEL
ZIEBACH
SULLY
HAND
BEADLE
KINGSBURY
BROOKINGS
LAWRENCE
MEADE
Pierre
HYDE
HUGHES
STANLEY
HAAKON
BUFFALO
JERAULD
SANBORN
MINER
LAKE
MOODY
PENNINGTON
JONES
LYMAN
BRULE
AURORA
HANSON
MCCOOK
MINNEHAHA
DAVISON
CUSTER
JACKSON
MELLETTE
DOUGLAS
HUTCHINSON
TURNER
LINCOLN
FALL RIVER
SHANNON
BENNETT
TODD
TRIPP
GREGORY
CHARLES MIX
BON HOMME
YANKTON
CLAY
UNION
Missouri

GOVERNMENT ON THE RESERVATIONS

Each of South Dakota's nine Indian tribes is its own nation with its own constitution. Voters choose their own government, made up of a tribal president (or chairperson) and council. The tribes also have their own courts. South Dakota's Office of Tribal Government Relations helps tribes pass laws that improve life on the reservations.

State Flag

The original state flag of South Dakota was designed and adopted in 1909. The flag features a field of blue with the state seal in the center. The state seal is surrounded by gold triangles representing the sun's rays. Surrounding the state seal is the inscription "South Dakota" on top and "The Mount Rushmore State" on the bottom. The text reading "The Mount Rushmore State" originally read "The Sunshine State," but it was changed in 1992.

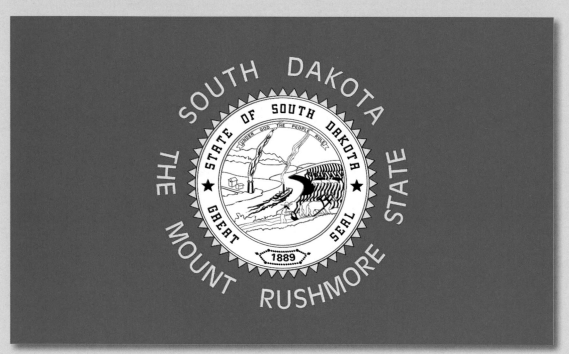

State Seal

The outer ring of the seal reads "State of South Dakota" on the top and "Great Seal" on the bottom. The outer ring also features the year of statehood, 1889. Inside the inner circle of the seal is the state motto, "Under God the People Rule." At the center of the seal is an image featuring hills, a river with a boat, a farmer, a mine, and cattle. These represent the state's industrial strength and natural resources.

READ ABOUT

Combines harvest
wheat on a South
Dakota farm.

CHAPTER EIGHT

ECONOMY

★

I N THE PAST, GETTING UP EARLY TO WORK THE FIELDS OR TAKE CARE OF LIVESTOCK WAS A WAY OF LIFE FOR MOST SOUTH DAKOTANS. Farming and ranching are still big business in the state, but the average worker is more likely to be found in a factory, office building, or store than on a farm. Whatever they do, South Dakotans work hard to help the state's economy grow.

A rancher rounds up a herd of cattle.

South Dakota ranks number one in the country for raising bison for meat. State ranchers own just over 38,500 head of bison.

FARMING AND RANCHING

For decades, the number of farms in South Dakota has dropped as the size of farms has grown. Meanwhile, new machinery has helped farmers grow more crops with fewer people. The crops grown have also changed. While corn and wheat are still important, soybeans and sunflowers are now also common. More than 4 million acres (1.6 million ha) of corn, the top crop, are planted each year, with more than 400 million bushels harvested annually. Nearly 100 million bushels of soybeans are harvested each year.

Ranching plays a huge part in South Dakota's farm economy as well. South Dakota's 17,000 ranchers produce about 3.7 million head of cattle each year, with cattle and

What Do South Dakotans Do?

This color-coded chart shows what industries South Dakotans work in.

24.2%	Educational services, and health care and social assistance 100,706
11.5%	Retail trade 47,921
9.9%	Manufacturing 41,157
9.2%	Arts, entertainment, and recreation, and accommodation and food services 38,227
7.3%	Finance and insurance, and real estate and rental and leasing 30,526
6.9%	Agriculture, forestry, fishing and hunting, and mining 28,929
6.5%	Construction 27,152
5.9%	Professional, scientific, and management, and administrative and waste management services 24,616
5.3%	Public administration 21,949
4.4%	Other services, except public administration 18,398
4.3%	Transportation and warehousing, and utilities 17,733
2.8%	Wholesale trade 11,777
1.8%	Information 7,596

Source: U.S. Census Bureau, 2010 census

calves the top product. South Dakota farmers also raise hogs, turkeys, sheep, and lambs. Some South Dakotans keep bees, and their honey is a valuable product, worth more than $33 million in 2012.

WEALTH FROM THE EARTH

Gold drew thousands of people to South Dakota's Black Hills in the 19th century, but today just one major gold mine remains open in the state. Rocks, stones, and clays used in construction are now the top nonfuel minerals produced in the state. These include Portland cement, sand and gravel, mica, and granite.

Top Products

Agriculture Cattle and calves, corn, grain, soybeans, wheat, chickens, dairy products, hay, sunflowers

Manufacturing Computer and electronics equipment, food processing, machinery, transportation equipment, fabricated metal products

Mining Granite, clay, limestone, crushed stone, sand, gravel, oil, gypsum, natural gas, gold

Major Agricultural and Mining Products

This map shows where South Dakota's major agricultural and mining products come from. See a cow? That means cattle are raised there.

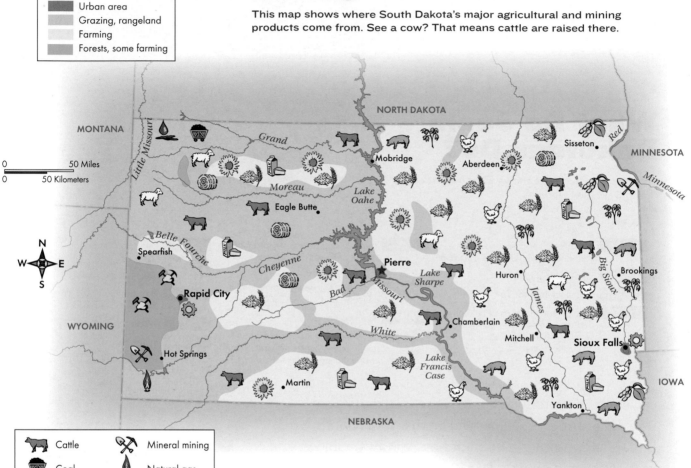

Urban area
Grazing, rangeland
Farming
Forests, some farming

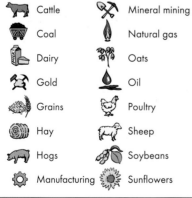

Cattle		Mineral mining
Coal		Natural gas
Dairy		Oats
Gold		Oil
Grains		Poultry
Hay		Sheep
Hogs		Soybeans
Manufacturing		Sunflowers

MAKING THINGS

Many South Dakotans who have moved to the city from the countryside have taken jobs in factories. The state's largest manufacturer is John Morrell & Company, which makes pork products. Its plant in Sioux Falls employs more than 3,000 workers. Daktronics, based in Brookings, makes scoreboards and electronic signs of all shapes and sizes. POET, with headquarters in Sioux Falls, is the nation's larg-

Many Native Americans earn a living by creating art related to their culture. Greg Red Elk is shown here with some of his acrylic paintings.

est producer of ethanol, an engine fuel made from corn and crop materials that remain after harvesting.

South Dakota is constantly recruiting new companies to come to the state. A leading business magazine named Sioux Falls as the best small city in the country for business. In 2013, Smith Company, a manufacturer of side-dump trailers, announced that it was moving its headquarters from Iowa to Elk Point. Permian, a Texas-based maker of storage tanks and processing equipment, will open new operations in Belle Fourche. Some people say South Dakota is the best state for entrepreneurs—people going into business for themselves. In recent years, companies that make things

SEE IT HERE!

SIOUX POTTERY

Not everything made in South Dakota comes from a farm or factory. See for yourself at Sioux Pottery in Rapid City. The artists are Lakotas. They specialize in making items out of red clay from the Black Hills. At the studio, you can meet the artists and watch them make pots, plates, Christmas ornaments, and other items.

ERNEST LAWRENCE: PRIZE-WINNING SCIENTIST

Physicist Ernest Lawrence (1901–1958) was born in Canton and graduated from the University of South Dakota in 1922. In 1930, he created the cyclotron, a circular device that speeds the movement of tiny particles of matter. The cyclotron helped Lawrence and other scientists study the tiniest particles known, and doctors have used beams of energy created by cyclotrons to treat cancer. For his work, Lawrence received science's highest award, the Nobel Prize in **Physics**. He is the only Nobel winner from South Dakota.

? Want to know more? Visit www.factsfor now.scholastic.com and enter the keywords **South Dakota**.

WORD TO KNOW

physics *the study of matter and energy*

Homestake Gold Mine is the deepest mine in the Western Hemisphere, plunging more than 8,000 feet (2,438 m) underground.

such as rifles and wind turbine blades have made plans to move to the state. The arrival of new companies means more jobs for construction workers. They build offices for the companies and new homes for people who work for them. Roughly 27,000 South Dakotans worked in construction in 2010.

SERVING OTHERS

Banking, selling goods, government work, and health care are just some parts of South Dakota's service economy. When it comes to putting people to work, the government is close to the top. More than 67,000 people work for some level of government in South Dakota—local, county, state, federal, or tribal.

Health care is a growing field in South Dakota, and Sanford Health is the largest nongovernment employer in the state, with more than 5,000 workers. Avera McKennan Hospital in Sioux Falls employs about 600 doctors, providing care in dozens of medical specialties. A major part of the service economy in South Dakota is tied to selling goods. Another important service is helping people take care of their money. Several large U.S. banks have operations in Sioux Falls that process credit card accounts for their customers.

Another service involves taking care of the several million tourists who visit South Dakota each year. In 2012, those guests spent more than $1.95 billion—money that

A doctor on the Pine Ridge Indian Reservation gives an Oglala Sioux boy a checkup.

helped create jobs for about 28,000 workers. Many tourists come to hunt and fish. Visitors also spend money on Indian reservations. Some come to enjoy nature, while others go to casinos. Tourism money helps reservation governments provide people with services.

MINI-BIO

T. DENNY SANFORD: BIG-TIME GIVER

As a young boy, T. Denny Sanford (1935—) got his first taste of the business world in his father's clothing company. After graduating from college in 1958, he started his own company, which sold construction products, and he later bought a chemical company.

In 1986, Sanford bought the United National Bank of Sioux Falls (now called First Premier Bank). In recent years, he has made many large donations to South Dakota organizations. The biggest came in 2007, when he gave $400 million to the Sioux Valley Hospitals and Health System. The company was renamed Sanford Health in his honor.

? Want to know more? Visit www.factsfor now.scholastic.com and enter the keywords **South Dakota**.

NORTH DAKOTA

MONTANA

MINNESOTA

N
W • E
S

Lemmon
Grand
Standing Rock Reservation
Kenel
Mobridge
Aberdeen
Sisseton
Eden
Roslyn
Waubay
Red

29

Castle Rock
Moreau
Eagle Butte
Lake Oahe
Gettysburg
Milbank
Watertown
Clear Lake

Belle Fourche
Belle Fourche
Cheyenne
Redfield
Miller
Big Sioux

Spearfish
Deadwood
Lead
Sturgis
Rapid City
Geographic Center of South Dakota
Pierre
De Smet
Brookings
Flandreau

Little Missouri

WYOMING

Black Hills National Forest
Keystone
Custer
Hot Springs
Wall
Philip
Bad
Murdo
Missouri
White
Lake Sharpe
Huron
Madison
Dell Rapids
Brandon

Interior
Badlands National Park
Mission
Winner
Chamberlain
Mitchell
Sioux Falls

90

James

90

229

Lake Francis Case
Pickstown
Yankton
Vermillion
N. Sioux City

29

IOWA

NEBRASKA

90 —— Interstate highway

0 ——— 50 Miles
0 ——— 50 Kilometers

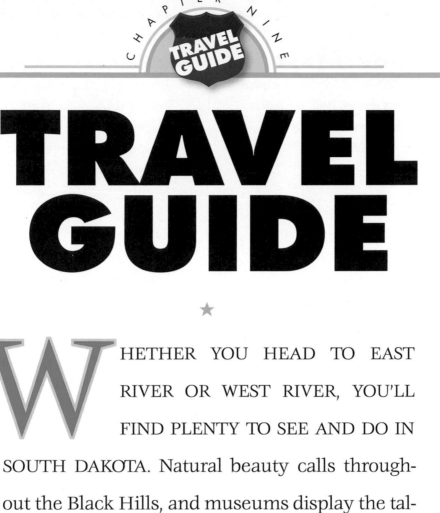

CHAPTER NINE

TRAVEL GUIDE

TRAVEL GUIDE

★

WHETHER YOU HEAD TO EAST RIVER OR WEST RIVER, YOU'LL FIND PLENTY TO SEE AND DO IN SOUTH DAKOTA. Natural beauty calls throughout the Black Hills, and museums display the talents of some of the state's best artists. Meanwhile, sites in Deadwood and elsewhere allow you to step into the state's past. With so much to see, you'll learn why some folks call South Dakota the Land of Infinite Variety!

←— Follow along with this travel map. We'll start our trip in Sioux Falls and end in Lemmon!

SOUTHEAST

THINGS TO DO: Take a musical trip through time, see Native American art, and go for a swim in Lewis and Clark Lake.

Sioux Falls

★ **Washington Pavilion of Arts and Science:** This facility includes a theater that features concerts and plays, a museum with all sorts of art, and the Kirby Science Discovery Center, where kids can learn about lasers, dinosaurs, weather, and much more.

★ **Great Plains Zoo:** More than 500 animals from around the world make their home at the Great Plains Zoo. They include wallabies from Australia, giraffes from Africa, and tortoises from South America. The zoo also has a natural history museum.

Feeding the goats at Great Plains Zoo

★ **Center for Western Studies:** Located at Augustana College, this center traces the history of the plains, from the Native American nations to Yankee and immigrant settlers. Displays range from Sioux clothing to furniture made by Norwegian immigrants.

★ **Falls Park:** At the center of this park are the waterfalls that gave Sioux Falls its name. A tower in the park gives a good view of the region, and you can walk along the remains of an old mill that was once powered by the rushing waters.

★ **USS *South Dakota* Battleship Memorial:** During World War II, sailors onboard the *South Dakota* fought all over the Pacific Ocean. Today, parts of the historic ship are on display at this memorial in Sherman Park. See for yourself just how big a 94-ton gun barrel is!

★ **Northern Plains Tribal Arts Expo:** For several days in September, Sioux Falls is home to a celebration of Native American art from across the Great Plains. Artists from 33 tribes display beadwork, paintings, and more. Saturday night features a powwow with dancing and drumming.

Lewis and Clark Recreation Area

Yankton

★ **Lewis and Clark Recreation Area:** Just outside of Yankton is Lewis and Clark Lake. At 22 miles (35 km) long, the lake offers plenty of water for boaters and swimmers. Around the lake are golf courses, campgrounds, bike trails, horse grounds—even an archery course.

★ **African Methodist Episcopal Church:** The first black church in Dakota Territory, this church is still being used today.

Mitchell

★ **Dakota Discovery Museum:** This museum displays a real bison skin tipi and a cabin like the ones homesteaders built to claim their own piece of South Dakota land. The museum also has works by Oscar Howe, Harvey Dunn, and other notable South Dakota artists.

SEE IT HERE!

NATIONAL MUSIC MUSEUM

At the National Music Museum, you won't just see it here—you'll hear it, too! As you walk among the hundreds of instruments, you can listen to a recording of some of them being played. Museum displays range from Asian flutes to electric guitars, and some of the instruments are hundreds of years old. Seeing them, you realize instruments can be beautiful works of art as well as tools to make equally beautiful music.

Guitars at the National Music Museum

★ **Enchanted World Doll Museum:** Inside this museum, which looks like a castle, are almost 5,000 dolls, some dating to the 1800s, and from more than 120 countries.

Vermillion

★ **W. H. Over Museum of Natural and Cultural History:** This museum includes displays about Native American and pioneer life and the natural history of South Dakota.

Pickstown

★ **Fort Randall Dam and Historic Site:** The Fort Randall Dam is one of several dams providing power to South Dakotans. You can tour the power plant and explore the nearby Fort Randall Historic Site. On the site are the remains of the army fort built there in 1856.

NORTHEAST

THINGS TO DO: Sample some sour food, imagine what it was like to be a pioneer child, and see thousands of birds at a wildlife refuge.

Brookings

★ **South Dakota Art Museum:** South Dakota's major art museum houses a large collection of works by Native American artists and painter Harvey Dunn. At the museum's Kids Sensation Station, young visitors can explore their own artistic talents.

Eden

★ **Fort Sisseton Historic State Park:** In pioneer days, soldiers at Fort Sisseton helped keep the peace between Native Americans and white settlers. Today, the remains

MINI-BIO

LAWRENCE DIGGS: THE VINEGAR MAN

At a tiny museum in Roslyn, near Eden, Lawrence Diggs (1948–) tells the world about the wonders of vinegar. Before coming to South Dakota, Diggs lived on several continents and served in the Peace Corps, which sends American volunteers to developing countries. He decided the small town of Roslyn was the perfect spot for a museum devoted to his favorite sour liquid. He studied how to make vinegar and cook with it. At his museum, Diggs shares his knowledge and displays paper made from vinegar.

❓ **Want to know more?** Visit www.factsfor now.scholastic.com and enter the keywords **South Dakota**.

of the fort give a glimpse into South Dakota's history. Many of the original buildings have been preserved or rebuilt, and guides dressed as 19th-century soldiers offer tours.

Soldiers reenacting daily life at Fort Sisseton

Ingalls Homestead

De Smet

★ **Ingalls Homestead:** Laura Ingalls Wilder wrote about her family's experiences on the South Dakota prairie. At this site, visitors can relive some of those experiences by exploring a dugout—a simple home built partially in the earth—or taking a ride in a covered wagon. There are also life-size models of the home and barn the Ingalls family built during the 1880s.

Waubay

★ **Waubay National Wildlife Refuge:** *Waubay* is Sioux for "a nesting place for birds." Today, about 100 kinds of birds nest in the refuge, and more than 240 species of birds spend at least part of the year there. They're attracted to habitats that range from forests to marshlands to prairie grasses.

Aberdeen

★ **Wylie Park:** This park includes typical activities such as camping, hiking, and sports. It also has a yellow brick road and people dressed as characters from *The Wizard of Oz.* Storybook Land features scenes from well-known folktales and songs, such as "There Was an Old Woman Who Lived in a Shoe" and "Jack and Jill."

★ **Dacotah Prairie Museum:** What's an elephant doing on the prairie? Amazing the visitors who come to this museum! The 11-foot-tall (3.4 m) beast is the largest of more than 50 mounted animals on display here. Others include a polar bear and a zebra. The museum also has exhibits on South Dakota art and history.

FAQ

Q8 WHAT'S THE CONNECTION BETWEEN ABERDEEN AND *THE WIZARD OF OZ*?

A8 L. Frank Baum, the author of more than a dozen books set in the land of Oz, lived in Aberdeen from 1888 to 1891. He ran a store and owned a newspaper.

CENTRAL SOUTH DAKOTA

THINGS TO DO: Learn more about some great South Dakotans, get your hands on a real bison hide, and admire Lakota art.

Chamberlain

★ **South Dakota Hall of Fame:** This museum highlights South Dakotans who made their mark in politics, sports, education, business, the arts, and other fields.

★ **Akta Lakota Museum & Cultural Center:** On the grounds of the St. Joseph Indian School is this museum dedicated to Lakota history. From life on the plains before Europeans arrived through today's efforts to preserve traditional culture, you'll learn it all here.

Akta Lakota Museum & Cultural Center

Medicine Rock at Dakota Sunset Museum

Gettysburg

★ **Dakota Sunset Museum:** This museum is the home of one big rock—it weighs about 40 tons. The big stone is called Medicine Rock. Several footprints are embedded in the rock, and no one is sure how they got there. The museum also has an old-time blacksmith shop.

Pierre

★ **South Dakota Discovery Center & Aquarium:** For hands-on science fun, the Discovery Center is the place to go. Kids can crawl through a life-size dinosaur nest or learn how to use lab equipment at the Imagination Station. The aquarium features fish found in the nearby Missouri River.

★ **Lake Oahe:** This lake was created when a dam was built along the Missouri River. Lake Oahe stretches out for 250 miles (402 km), providing plenty of recreational activities. Fishing is a major sport, with walleye the main catch.

★ **Lewis and Clark Family Center:** Located at the Farm Island Recreation Area, this center is full of hands-on fun. Feel real elk and bison skins, or sit inside a dugout canoe, the kind used by Indians and trappers centuries ago. You can also learn more about the experiences of Lewis and Clark as they traveled through South Dakota.

SEE IT HERE!

CULTURAL HERITAGE CENTER

Want to explore all of South Dakota's history in one spot? Then the state historical society's Cultural Heritage Center in Pierre is the place to go. The museum is the largest in the state and features more than 1,300 items relating to Sioux history—including a life-size tipi. You can also see a life-size sod house and exhibits and documents describing South Dakota from settler days to the present.

Mobridge

★ **Klein Museum:** Step into the old country schoolhouse at this museum—just one sample of life on the frontier in pioneer days. The museum also has examples of Lakota art.

Standing Rock Reservation

★ **Sitting Bull and Sacagawea Monuments:** Overlooking the Missouri River is a marker showing the spot where the great Lakota chief Sitting Bull is said to be buried. South Dakota artist Korczak Ziolkowski created the sculpture of the chief's head that tops the marker. Another monument nearby honors Sacagawea, the Shoshone woman who traveled with Lewis and Clark on their expedition.

Sitting Bull monument and grave site

FAQ

Q: HOW DID MOBRIDGE GET ITS NAME?

A: When a bridge over the Missouri River went up in 1906, a telegraph operator used the abbreviation for Missouri—MO—to describe the location. That created the word Mobridge and the name of a new South Dakota town.

Kenel

★ **Fort Manuel Lisa:** Manuel Lisa helped create South Dakota's fur trade, and the fort named for him is a life-size model of the one he built outside Kenel in 1811. According to some reports, Sacagawea died at about age 25 at the original fort; the new one has an exhibit about her life.

Murdo

★ **Pioneer Auto Museum and Antique Town:** Want to see one of the world's few eight-wheeled cars? Then head to this museum, which has about 250 cars, trucks, and motorcycles—some more than 100 years old. Other collections include pedal cars, toys, bikes—even doorknobs!

THE BADLANDS AND THE BLACK HILLS

THINGS TO DO: Get close to some big bones, take an elevator ride underground, and journey into the past.

Mission

★ **Sicangu Heritage Center:** On the Rosebud Sioux Reservation, this museum tracks the history of the Sicangu (Brulé) Lakota. The exhibits include quilts and spectacular feather headdresses.

Interior

★ **Badlands National Park:** Covering 381 square miles (987 sq km), this national park features some of the most colorful eroded hills and gullies of the Badlands region. Hikers might see bison, bighorn sheep, or swift foxes.

Badlands National Park

★ **Minuteman Missile National Historic Site:** Take an elevator ride underground to see where members of the U.S. Air Force once sat ready in case they ever got an order to fire missiles. The Minuteman site traces the role South Dakota played during the cold war.

Sturgis

★ **Motorcycle Museum & Hall of Fame:** Since 2001, Sturgis has been home to the Motorcycle Museum & Hall of Fame, which displays some motorcycles that are more than 100 years old.

Deadwood

★ **Days of '76 Museum:** This museum honors the Days of '76 Rodeo, which has been held since 1923. Real stagecoaches and horse-drawn carriages are on display, along with photos from the rodeos.

★ **Tatanka—Story of the Bison:** At the heart of this site is a series of large sculptures showing three Native Americans on horseback hunting 14 bison. The site also has a tipi and Lakotas in traditional clothing who explain their people's long relationship with bison.

Adams Museum

★ **Adams Museum:** The oldest museum in the Black Hills features a copy of the gold nugget—found by local legend "Potato Creek" Johnny—said to be one of the largest ever uncovered in the area. The real nugget, weighing just under 8 ounces (227 grams), is locked up in the museum. You can also see guns that once belonged to Wild Bill Hickok.

Rapid City

★ **The Journey Museum:** Take a journey to the past, when dinosaurs once roamed the Black Hills. The museum traces the region's history from those ancient days right up to the present.

An albino python at Reptile Gardens

★ **Reptile Gardens:** This site is home to the largest reptile collection in the world. From huge alligators to deadly snakes, they're all here.

★ **South Dakota Air and Space Museum:** Located on the Ellsworth Air Force Base, this museum lets you get close to some of the best fighter planes ever flown. You can even feel what it's like to fly some of these jets!

Lead

★ **Black Hills Mining Museum:** Get your hands wet, just like the miners of old, at this museum. You can pan for tiny nuggets of gold as well as learn about the history of mining in the Black Hills.

★ **Homestake Mine Tour:** Gold made Lead a boomtown, and today, you can visit sites where gold was once processed. At the end of your visit, you'll get your own small nugget of gold taken from local mines.

Wall

★ **Wounded Knee Museum:** The museum covers this painful part of Lakota history in great detail, from the arrival of the Ghost Dancers to the massacre itself.

SEE IT HERE!

WALL DRUG

A stuffed jackrabbit topped with antelope horns—South Dakotans call it a jackalope—is just one of the odd items for sale at Wall Drug. What once was a tiny drugstore has grown into a major tourist stop, thanks to humorous signs for the store posted all over South Dakota. The first signs for Wall Drug offered free cold water to anyone who came by. Today, the store is famous for its homemade doughnuts and robotic singing cowboys, as well as souvenirs of all kinds.

Spearfish

★ **D. C. Booth National Historic Fish Hatchery:** This **hatchery** is one of the oldest in the country. It features a museum and an underwater viewing area where visitors can see some of the fish hatched there.

WORD TO KNOW

hatchery *a place where eggs of fish or other animals are hatched in large numbers*

Custer

★ **Black Hills National Forest:** This national forest is more than just trees. It also has caves, lakes, grasslands, and mountains. South Dakota's highest spot, Harney Peak, is in the forest, and a tower on top of it offers a view of neighboring states, as well as the Black Hills themselves.

★ **Custer State Park:** About 1,500 bison roam this state park, along with pronghorn, bighorn sheep, and mountain goats. The park offers miles of trails and beautiful camping sites, as well as five lakes. Rock climbers come to scale the Needles, long, thin columns of granite that shoot up from the forests.

★ **Crazy Horse Memorial:** Since 1948, workers have been carving a huge statue of the Lakota leader Crazy Horse in the Black Hills, just north of Custer. Today, the face is complete, and work continues on his long, outstretched arm. The site also has a museum and cultural center where you can learn more about Native American history.

★ **Four Mile Old West Town:** Stagecoaches once stopped at this spot 4 miles (6 km) outside of Custer, which led to its name. Today, Four Mile shows what a typical frontier town looked like, with its saloon, general store, and jails. You can still see some grooves cut into the ground by horse-drawn wagons. Actors play the part of original settlers and help explain the history of Four Mile.

Bighorn sheep at Custer State Park

★ **Jewel Cave National Monument:**
At just over 141 miles (227 km),
Jewel is the third-longest cave in the
world. Visitors can explore part of
the cave and learn about its crystals
and other rock formations.

Hot Springs

★ **Wind Cave National Park:** More
than 100 miles (160 km) of underground caves and passages are at
the heart of this national park.

★ **Black Hills Wild Horse
Sanctuary:** Just outside of Hot
Springs, herds of wild horses roam
freely, as they did across the Great
Plains hundreds of years ago.
Visitors can see ancient Native
American rock carvings.

Mustangs at Black Hills Wild Horse Sanctuary

SEE IT HERE!

MAMMOTH SITE MUSEUM

More than 25,000 years ago, the Black Hills were home
to mammoths, relatives of today's elephants. Today, at this
site in Hot Springs, archaeologists still work to uncover
the bones of these creatures, which grew to a height of
14 feet (4.3 m). The remains of 55 mammoths have been
found. Visitors can walk among the partially uncovered
bones, or head into the exhibition hall to see a life-size
model of a complete mammoth.

Keystone

★ **National Presidential Wax
Museum:** All the U.S. presidents—
or at least wax versions of them—
are in Keystone. These life-size
sculptures depict the leaders in historic scenes, and recordings provide
details about their lives.

★ **Mount Rushmore National
Memorial:** This massive granite
sculpture, near Keystone, fea-
tures four U.S. presidents: George
Washington, Thomas Jefferson,
Theodore Roosevelt, and Abraham
Lincoln. More than 2 million people
visit the site each year.

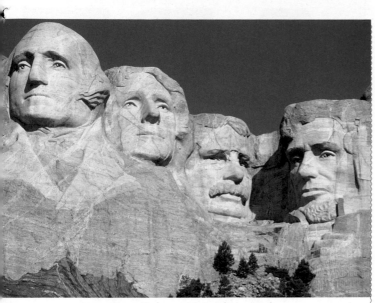
Mount Rushmore National Memorial

★ **Borglum Historical Center:**
Gutzon Borglum won acclaim for
creating Mount Rushmore; this
center gives the complete story of
his life and art.

NORTHWEST CORNER

**THINGS TO DO: See wood
that has turned to rock or
learn about rodeos.**

Belle Fourche

★ **Tri-State Museum:** This museum
honors the shared history of South
Dakota and the neighboring parts of
Wyoming and Montana. The focus is
on pioneer days and rodeos.

★ **Geographic Center of the Nation
Monument:** When Alaska and
Hawai'i entered the United States
in 1959, the geographic center of
the country shifted to a site within
South Dakota. In 2007, Belle Fourche
officials put down a huge concrete
and bronze monument to mark that
honor. The actual spot is about 20
miles (32 km) north of Belle Fourche
on old Highway 85. A small marker
there shows the U.S. government's
best guess of the exact center.

Lemmon

★ **Petrified Wood Park and
Museum:** Petrified wood is ancient
wood that has turned rock-hard over
time. Lemmon claims to have the
world's largest park and museum
devoted to petrified wood. One of
the attractions is a giant castle made
of petrified wood and petrified dinosaur and mammoth bones.

★ **Grand River Museum:** There's
a little something for everyone at
this museum, from dinosaur bones
to exhibits on ranching to the giant
sculptures that local artist John
Lopez made from scrap metal.
Sitting Bull and a *T. rex* are just two
of the subjects Lopez captured in
metal.

WRITING PROJECTS

Check out these ideas for creating a campaign brochure and writing you-are-there narratives. Or research the lives of famous people from South Dakota.

118

ART PROJECTS

You can illustrate the state song, create a dazzling PowerPoint presentation, or learn about the state quarter and design your own.

119

TIMELINE

What happened when? This timeline highlights important events in the state's history—and shows what was happening throughout the United States at the same time.

122

GLOSSARY

Remember the Words to Know from the chapters in this book? They're all collected here.

125

FAST FACTS

Use this section to find fascinating facts about state symbols, land area and population statistics, weather, sports teams, and much more.

126

SCIENCE, TECHNOLOGY, ENGINEERING, & MATH PROJECTS

Make weather maps, graph population statistics, and research endangered species that live in the state.

120

PRIMARY VS. SECONDARY SOURCES

121

So what are primary and secondary sources? And what's the diff? This section explains all that and where you can find them.

BIOGRAPHICAL DICTIONARY

133

This at-a-glance guide highlights some of the state's most important and influential people. Visit this section and read about their contributions to the state, the country, and the world.

RESOURCES

Books and much more. Take a look at these additional sources for information about the state.

138

WRITING PROJECTS

Write a Memoir, Journal, or Editorial for Your School Newspaper!

Picture Yourself . . .

★ As a child growing up in a Lakota camp. How would your responsibilities change and expand as you grow older? Would there be different responsibilities for boys and girls? What would everyday life be like?

SEE: Chapter Two, page 30.

★ Moving with your family to the South Dakota prairie. Write journal entries describing what life is like. How do you build a sod house? Where do you find food? How do you keep warm?

SEE: Chapter Four, pages 50–52.

Create an Election Brochure or Web Site!

Run for office! Throughout this book, you've read about some of the issues that concern South Dakota today. As a candidate for governor of South Dakota, create a campaign brochure or Web site.

★ Explain how you meet the qualifications to be governor of South Dakota.

★ Talk about the three or four major issues you'll focus on if you're elected.

★ Remember, you'll be responsible for South Dakota's budget. How would you spend the taxpayers' money?

SEE: Chapter Seven, pages 86–88.

Create an interview script with a famous person from South Dakota!

★ Research various South Dakotans, such as Sitting Bull, Mamie Shields Pyle, Joe Foss, Russell Means, Laura Ingalls Wilder, Oscar Howe, Oscar Micheaux, Billy Mills, Tom Brokaw, Mary Hart, and others.

★ Based on your research, pick one person you would most like to talk with.

★ Write a script of the interview. What questions would you ask? How would this person answer? Create a question-and-answer format. You may want to supplement this writing project with a voice-recording dramatization of the interview.

SEE: Chapters Four, Five, and Six, pages 48, 56, 63, 66, 78, 79, 80, 81, and the Biographical Dictionary, pages 133–137.

ART PROJECTS

Create a PowerPoint Presentation or Visitors' Guide

Welcome to South Dakota!

South Dakota's a great place to visit and to live! From its natural beauty to its historical sites, there's plenty to see and do. In your PowerPoint presentation or brochure, highlight 10 to 15 of South Dakota's fascinating landmarks. Be sure to include:

★ a map of the state showing where these sites are located

★ photos, illustrations, Web links, natural history facts, geographic stats, climate and weather, plants and wildlife, and recent discoveries

SEE: Chapter Nine, pages 102–115, and Fast Facts, pages 126–127.

Illustrate the Lyrics to the South Dakota State Song

("Hail! South Dakota")

Use markers, paints, photos, collages, colored pencils, or computer graphics to illustrate the lyrics to "Hail! South Dakota." Turn your illustrations into a picture book, or scan them into PowerPoint and add music.

SEE: The lyrics to "Hail! South Dakota" on page 128.

Research South Dakota's State Quarter

From 1999 to 2008, the U.S. Mint introduced new quarters commemorating each of the 50 states in the order that they were admitted to the Union. Each state's quarter features a unique design on its reverse, or back.

★ Research the significance of the image. Who designed the quarter? Who chose the final design?

★ Design your own South Dakota quarter. What images would you choose for the reverse?

★ Make a poster showing the South Dakota quarter and label each image.

GO TO: www.factsfornow.scholastic.com. Enter the keywords **South Dakota** and look for the link to the South Dakota quarter.

SCIENCE, TECHNOLOGY, ENGINEERING, & MATH PROJECTS

Graph Population Statistics!

★ Compare population statistics (such as ethnic background, birth, death, and literacy rates) in South Dakota counties or major cities. In your graph or chart, look at population density and write sentences describing what the population statistics show; graph one set of population statistics and write a paragraph explaining what the graphs reveal.

SEE: Chapter Six, pages 72–75.

Create a Weather Map of South Dakota!

Use your knowledge of South Dakota geography to research and identify conditions that result in specific weather events. What is it about the geography of South Dakota that makes it vulnerable to things like blizzards? Create a weather map or poster that shows the weather patterns over the state. Include a caption explaining the technology used to measure weather phenomena and provide data.

SEE: Chapter One, pages 15–16.

Track Endangered Species

Using your knowledge of South Dakota's wildlife, research which animals and plants are endangered or threatened.

★ Find out what the state is doing to protect these species.

★ Chart known populations of the animals and plants, and report on changes in certain geographic areas.

SEE: Chapter One, page 19.

Whooping crane

PRIMARY VS. SECONDARY SOURCES

What's the Diff?

Your teacher may require at least one or two primary sources and one or two secondary sources for your assignment. So, what's the difference between the two?

★ **Primary sources are original.** You are reading the actual words of someone's diary, journal, letter, autobiography, or interview. Primary sources can also be photographs, maps, prints, cartoons, news/film footage, posters, first-person newspaper articles, drawings, musical scores, and recordings. By the way, when you conduct a survey, interview someone, shoot a video, or take photographs to include in a project, you are creating primary sources!

★ **Secondary sources are what you find in encyclopedias, textbooks, articles, biographies, and almanacs.** These are written by a person or group of people who tell about something that happened to someone else. Secondary sources also recount what another person said or did. This book is an example of a secondary source.

Now that you know what primary sources are—where can you find them?

★ **Your school or local library:** Check the library catalog for collections of original writings, government documents, musical scores, and so on. Some of this material may be stored on microfilm.

★ **Historical societies:** These organizations keep historical documents, photographs, and other materials. Staff members can help you find what you are looking for. History museums are also great places to see primary sources firsthand.

★ **The Internet:** There are lots of sites that have primary sources you can download and use in a project or assignment.

TIMELINE

★ ★ ★

U.S. Events | c. 10,000 BCE | **South Dakota Events**

c. 10,000 BCE
Native people hunt mammoths in what is now South Dakota.

| c. 500 BCE |

c. 500 CE
Mound Builders arrive in South Dakota.

| c. 1000 |

c. 1000
Pre-Arikaras arrive in the region.

| c. 1300 |

c. 1300–mid-1500s
Arikaras arrive in South Dakota.

| 1600 |

c. 1600
Arikaras begin trading for European goods.

1607
The first permanent English settlement in North America is established at Jamestown.

| 1700 |

1700s
A smallpox epidemic kills thousands of Arikaras.

Mid-1700s
Sioux come to South Dakota from Minnesota.

1743
The La Vérendrye brothers are the first known European explorers in South Dakota.

1776
Thirteen American colonies declare their independence from Great Britain.

1787
The U.S. Constitution is written.

| 1800 |

1803
The Louisiana Purchase almost doubles the size of the United States.

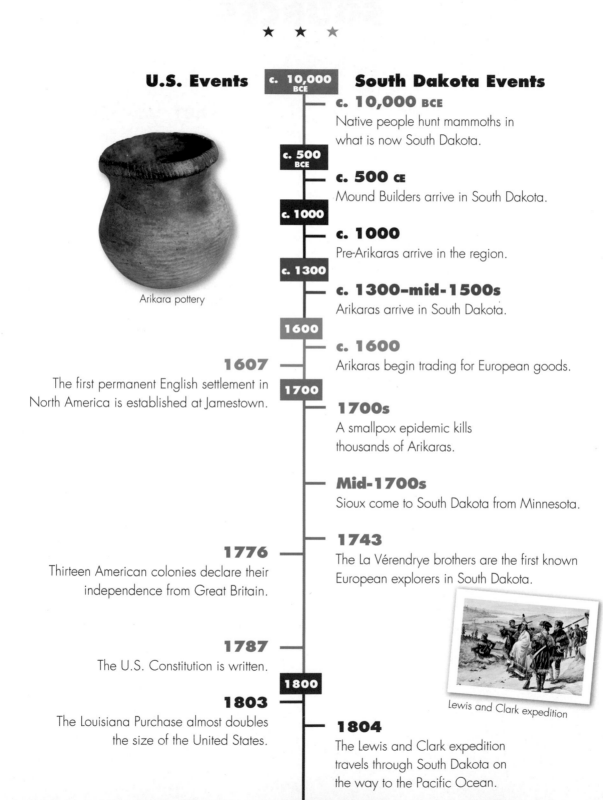

Arikara pottery

Lewis and Clark expedition

1804
The Lewis and Clark expedition travels through South Dakota on the way to the Pacific Ocean.

U.S. Events

1812-15

The United States and Great Britain fight the War of 1812.

1830

The Indian Removal Act forces eastern Native American groups to relocate west of the Mississippi River.

1861-65

The American Civil War is fought between the Northern Union and the Southern Confederacy; it ends with the surrender of the Confederate army, led by General Robert E. Lee.

1886

Apache leader Geronimo surrenders to the U.S. Army, ending the last major Native American rebellion against the expansion of the United States into the West.

1917-18

The United States engages in World War I.

1920

The Nineteenth Amendment to the U.S. Constitution grants women the right to vote.

South Dakota Events

Early 1800s

The fur trade thrives in South Dakota.

1851

Lakotas and other Great Plains nations sign a treaty promising peaceful relations.

1856

Sioux Falls, the first permanent European American town in South Dakota, is founded.

1861

The U.S. government creates the Dakota Territory.

1874

George Custer leads a military expedition that finds gold in the Black Hills.

1876

Lakotas fight to defend their lands.

1878-87

Thousands of homesteaders claim land during the Dakota land boom.

1889

South Dakota becomes the 40th state.

1890

U.S. troops kill about 350 Lakotas at the Wounded Knee Massacre.

1900

Wounded Knee Massacre

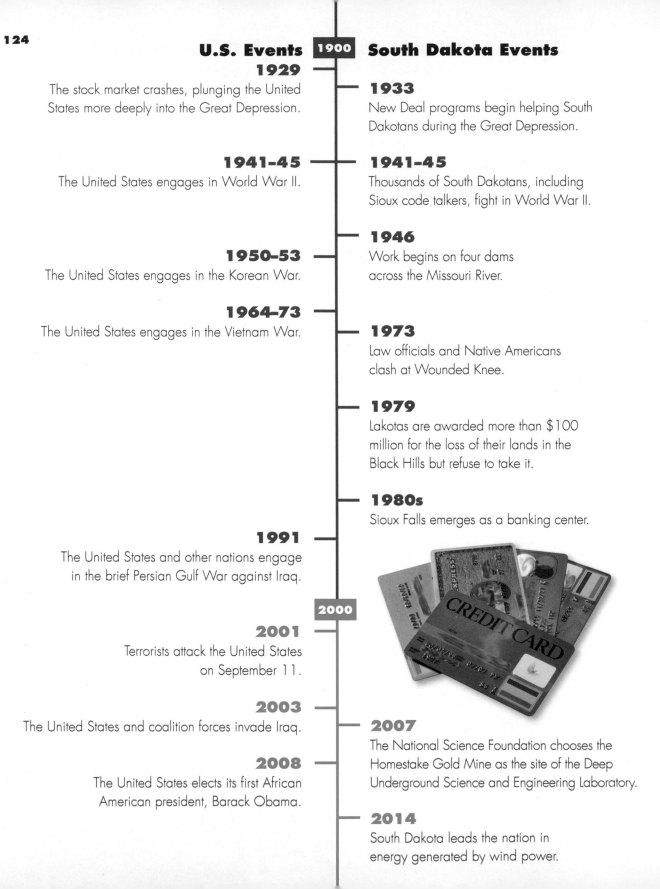

124

1929
The stock market crashes, plunging the United States more deeply into the Great Depression.

1933
New Deal programs begin helping South Dakotans during the Great Depression.

1941–45
The United States engages in World War II.

1941–45
Thousands of South Dakotans, including Sioux code talkers, fight in World War II.

1946
Work begins on four dams across the Missouri River.

1950–53
The United States engages in the Korean War.

1964–73
The United States engages in the Vietnam War.

1973
Law officials and Native Americans clash at Wounded Knee.

1979
Lakotas are awarded more than $100 million for the loss of their lands in the Black Hills but refuse to take it.

1980s
Sioux Falls emerges as a banking center.

1991
The United States and other nations engage in the brief Persian Gulf War against Iraq.

`2000`

2001
Terrorists attack the United States on September 11.

2003
The United States and coalition forces invade Iraq.

2007
The National Science Foundation chooses the Homestake Gold Mine as the site of the Deep Underground Science and Engineering Laboratory.

2008
The United States elects its first African American president, Barack Obama.

2014
South Dakota leads the nation in energy generated by wind power.

GLOSSARY

★ ★ ★

allies people who are on the same side in a conflict

anthropologist a person who studies the development of human cultures

archaeologists people who study the remains of past human societies

constitution a written document that contains all the governing principles of a state or country

endangered at risk of becoming extinct

erosion the wearing away of land by water, ice, wind, and other factors

expedition a trip for the purpose of exploration

glaciers slow-moving masses of ice

hatchery a place where eggs of fish or other animals are hatched in large numbers

irrigation watering land by artificial means to promote plant growth

missionary a person who tries to convert others to a religion

naturalist a person who studies natural history

ordinances laws passed by local governments

petition a formal written request signed by a group of voters

physics the study of matter and energy

plateau an elevated part of the earth with steep slopes

precipitation all water that falls to the earth, including rain, sleet, hail, snow, dew, fog, or mist

reservoirs artificial lakes or tanks for storing water

Scandinavia a region of northern Europe made up of Sweden, Norway, Denmark, Finland, and Iceland

shelterbelts rows of trees that provide shelter from the wind

sod soil thickly packed together with grass and roots

turbines machines for making power through the rotation of blades powered by wind, water, or steam

FAST FACTS

★ ★ ★

State Symbols

Statehood date	November 2, 1889, the 40th state
Origin of state name	From the Sioux word for "friend"
State capital	Pierre
State nickname	Coyote State, Mount Rushmore State
State motto	"Under God the People Rule"
State bird	Ring-necked pheasant
State flower	American pasque
State grass	Western wheatgrass
State soil	Houdek soil
State animal	Coyote
State fish	Walleye
State insect	Honeybee
State fossil	Triceratops
State mineral	Rose quartz
State gemstone	Fairburn agate
State jewelry	Black Hills gold
State song	"Hail! South Dakota"
State tree	Black Hills spruce
State fair	Late August–September at Huron

State seal

Geography

Total area; rank	77,116 square miles (199,730 sq km); 17th
Land; rank	75,811 square miles (196,350 sq km); 16th
Water; rank	1,305 square miles (3,380 sq km); 29th
Inland water; rank	1,305 square miles (3,380 sq km); 17th
Geographic center	Hughes, 8 miles (13 km) northeast of Pierre
Latitude	42°29'30" N to 45°56' N
Longitude	98°28'33" W to 104°3' W
Highest point	Harney Peak, 7,242 feet (2,207 m), in Pennington County
Lowest point	Big Stone Lake, 966 feet (294 m), in Roberts County

Largest city Sioux Falls
Number of counties 66
Longest river Missouri River

Population

Population; rank (2010 census) 814,180; 46th
Density (2010 census) 11 persons per square mile (4 per sq km)
Population distribution (2010 census) 57% urban, 43% rural
Ethnic distribution (2010 census) White persons: 84.7%
American Indian and Alaska Native persons: 8.5%
Persons of Hispanic or Latino origin: 2.7%
Persons reporting two or more races: 1.8%
Black persons: 1.2%
Asian persons: 0.9%
Persons of some other race: 0.1%

Weather

Record high temperature 120°F (49°C) at Gann Valley on July 5, 1936
and at Fort Pierre on July 15, 2006
Record low temperature −58°F (−50°C) at McIntosh on February 17, 1936
Average July temperature, Sioux Falls 73°F (23°C)
Average January temperature, Sioux Falls 17°F (−8°C)
Average yearly precipitation, Sioux Falls 16 inches (41 cm)

State flag

STATE SONG

★ ★ ★

"Hail! South Dakota"

DeeCort Hammitt wrote the words and music to this march. It officially became the state song in 1943.

Hail! South Dakota, A great state of the land,
Health, wealth and beauty, That's what makes her grand;
She has her Black Hills, And mines with gold so rare,
And with her scenery, No other state can compare.

Come where the sun shines, And where life's worth your
while,
You won't be here long, 'Till you'll wear a smile;
No state's so healthy, And no folk quite so true,
To South Dakota. We welcome you.

Hail! South Dakota, The state we love the best,
Land of our fathers, Builders of the west;
Home of the Badlands, and Rushmore's ageless shrine,
Black Hills and prairies, Farmland and Sunshine.
Hills, farms and prairies, Blessed with bright Sunshine.

NATURAL AREAS AND HISTORIC SITES

★ ★ ★

National Park

Badlands National Park features spectacular landscapes of eroded buttes, pinnacles, and spires.

Wind Cave National Park preserves one of the world's longest and most complex caves. The park also serves as a habitat for bison, elk, mule deer, and coyotes.

National Monument

Jewel Cave National Monument is the third-longest cave system in the world.

National Memorial

Mount Rushmore National Memorial shows the carved faces of George Washington, Thomas Jefferson, Theodore Roosevelt, and Abraham Lincoln.

National Recreational River

Meandering into South Dakota is the *Missouri National Recreational River*, which is a great place to see eagles, hawks, beavers, turtles, deer, and foxes.

National Historic Site

South Dakota's *Minuteman Missile National Historic Site* is home to a launch control facility and a missile silo complex.

National Historic Trail

Lewis & Clark National Historic Trail passes through South Dakota, following the route of Lewis and Clark's journey.

National Forest

South Dakota has one national forest, the *Black Hills National Forest,* which covers an area of more than 1.2 million acres (486,000 ha) and features Harney Peak, the tallest mountain in South Dakota and the highest peak east of the Rocky Mountains in the United States.

State Parks and Forests

South Dakota's state park system features and maintains 63 state park and recreation areas, including *Custer State Park*, *George S. Mickelson Trail*, and *Palisades State Park*.

SPORTS TEAMS

★ ★ ★

NCAA Teams (Division I)

Augustana College *Vikings*
Northern State University *Wolves*
South Dakota State University *Jackrabbits*
University of South Dakota *Coyotes*

A matchup between South Dakota State and North
Dakota State men's basketball teams

CULTURAL INSTITUTIONS

★ ★ ★

Libraries

The *University of South Dakota Library* (Vermillion) and the South Dakota State University Library (Brookings) have the major academic collections in the state.

The *Sioux Falls Public Library* is the largest public library in the state, with special collections on art and the history of South Dakota.

The *Library of the South Dakota State Historical Society* holds extensive collections on the history of the state.

Museums

The *Museum of Geology* at the South Dakota School of Mines and Technology (Rapid City) contains exhibits on the geology of South Dakota.

The *Sioux Indian Museum* (Rapid City) and the *W. H. Over Museum of Natural and Cultural History* (Vermillion) have collections related to American Indian heritage and history.

The *Cultural Heritage Center* (Pierre) contains displays of historical, military, and Indian artifacts that portray the life and culture of South Dakota from the days of the Plains Indians to modern times.

Performing Arts

The *Black Hills Symphony Orchestra* (Rapid City) stages a variety of concerts throughout the year, from chamber music to classical concerts to rock and roll tribute shows.

The *South Dakota Symphony Orchestra* (Sioux Falls), founded in 2000, puts on orchestra concerts, chamber concerts, and special events shows at the Washington Pavilion of Arts and Science.

Universities and Colleges

In 2011, South Dakota had 7 public and 12 private institutions of higher learning.

ANNUAL EVENTS

January–March

Black Hills Stock Show and Rodeo in Rapid City (January–February)

Schmeckfest in Freeman (late March/ early April)

April–June

Kids Fishing Weekend in Pierre (May)

Czech Days in Tabor (June)

Fort Sisseton Historical Festival in Fort Sisseton Historic State Park (June)

ICS Chili Cook-off in Belle Fourche (June)

Spring Arabian Horse Shows in Sioux Falls (April)

Laura Ingalls Wilder Pageant in De Smet (late June/early July)

July–September

Wall Celebration in Wall (July)

Black Hills Roundup in Belle Fourche (July)

Sitting Bull Stampede in Mobridge (July)

Gold Discovery Days in Custer (July)

Summer Arts Festival in Brookings (July)

Days of '76 Rodeo in Deadwood (July)

Corn Palace Festival in Mitchell (August)

Selby Area Rodeo (August)

Lewis and Clark Sprint Triathlon in Chamberlain (August)

Sturgis Motorcycle Rally (August)

Sioux Empire Fair in Sioux Falls (August)

State Fair in Huron (late August/early September)

Mickelson Trail Trek in Lead (September)

Buffalo Roundup & Arts Festival in Custer State Park (September/October)

October–December

Festival of Trees in Sioux Falls (November)

Parade of Lights in Pierre (November)

Christmas at the Capitol in Pierre (November/ December)

George Lee "Sparky" Anderson (1934–2010), a native of Bridgewater, was one of the most successful baseball managers in history. His teams won three World Series, and he was elected to the National Baseball Hall of Fame.

Jesse Bail (1979–) is a rodeo star who excels at riding bulls and broncos—especially hard-to-ride horses. In 2000, he was the college all-around rodeo champion. He was born in Spearfish.

Bob Barker (1923–) spent most of his early life on South Dakota's Rosebud Reservation, where his mother was a teacher. He went on to become a TV star, hosting the game show *The Price Is Right* for 35 years.

Nicholas Black Elk (1863–1950), an Oglala Lakota medicine man and cousin of Crazy Horse, fought at the Battle of the Little Bighorn. He gave a series of interviews about his life and Sioux culture that became a best-selling book, *Black Elk Speaks*.

Gutzon Borglum (1867–1941) was born in Idaho and created a sculpture of Abraham Lincoln that now stands in the Capitol in Washington, D.C., before coming to South Dakota to begin his greatest work, Mount Rushmore. He had a team of workers who carried out his vision for carving the heads of four U.S. presidents out of rock.

Gutzon Borglum

Tom Brokaw (1940–), a TV journalist born in Webster, reported from the White House for NBC News and then served as the anchor for that network's nightly news broadcast.

Martha Jane Cannary (Calamity Jane) (c. 1852–1903) came to Deadwood when it was a booming gold town. She dressed as a man, worked as a scout, and adapted to the rough life on the frontier.

Pierre Chouteau Jr. (1789–1865), the son of a successful trader, followed in his father's footsteps. He built Fort Pierre, which gave its name to the nearby city, and brought the first steamboat up the Missouri River to South Dakota.

Charles Badger Clark (1883–1957) was the first state poet of South Dakota. Born in Iowa, he moved to the Black Hills region in 1925, where he lived in a log cabin for 30 years.

Shawn Colvin (1956–), born in Vermillion, is a singer-songwriter who has won three Grammy Awards. She is best known for her hit song "Sunny Came Home."

Tom Brokaw

Crazy Horse (1849–1877) was one of the bravest Sioux leaders. He fought hard to keep settlers out of Lakota lands and to preserve the traditional Sioux way of life.

Tom Daschle (1947–), a native of Aberdeen and a graduate of South Dakota State University, was a U.S. senator from the state from 1987 to 2005.

Dennis Daugaard See page 89.

Ella Deloria See page 29.

Vine Deloria Jr. (1933–2005) was a writer and teacher who spoke out strongly for Indian rights and, for a time, led the National Congress of American Indians.

Pierre-Jean De Smet (1801–1873), a native of Belgium, was a priest who came to the United States in 1821 and arrived in South Dakota in 1839. During the 1860s, he spent time in the Badlands with the Lakota Nation, helping them maintain peaceful relations with European settlers.

Pete Dexter (1943–), a graduate of the University of South Dakota, was a reporter before becoming a prize-winning novelist. One of his earliest books explores the history of Deadwood.

Tom Daschle

Lawrence Diggs See page 106.

Harvey Dunn (1884–1952), who was born on a South Dakota homestead, was a painter and illustrator. Much of his work is now on display in South Dakota museums.

Charles Eastman (1858–1939) was a doctor who was part Santee Dakota. He wrote several books about his life as a Sioux and worked to improve the rights of all Native Americans.

Joe Foss See page 63.

Terry Francona (1959–) is a former baseball player and a current major league manager. As manager of the Boston Red Sox in 2004, he led the team to its first World Series championship in 86 years. He was born in Aberdeen.

Archer Gilfillan (1886–1955) spent almost two decades as a sheepherder in South Dakota and then wrote about his experiences in a best-selling book, *Sheep: Life on the South Dakota Range.*

Pete Dexter

Mary Hart

Mary Hart (1950–), a former Miss South Dakota, has had a long career in TV, much of it as the co-host of *Entertainment Tonight*. She was born in Madison.

Linda M. Hasselstrom See page 21.

"Wild Bill" Hickok (1837–1876) was a sheriff and gunfighter who was killed in Deadwood while playing poker.

Oscar Howe (1915–1983), born on the Crow Creek Sioux Reservation, was a Yanktonai Dakota artist, whose colorful, dynamic art was displayed in shows throughout the world.

Hubert Humphrey (1911–1978), a native of Wallace, later moved to Minnesota and entered politics. He served as the vice president of the United States from 1965 to 1969 and was the Democratic nominee for president in 1968.

Abbie Jarvis (1854–1931) was South Dakota's first female doctor and helped deliver more than 600 babies.

Tim Johnson (1946–), a Canton native, has represented South Dakota in the U.S. Senate since 1997.

Jason Kubel (1982–) is a professional baseball player who has played for the Minnesota Twins, the Arizona Diamondbacks, and the Cleveland Indians. In 2012, the hard-hitting designated hitter slugged 30 home runs. He is from Belle Fourche.

Cheryl Ladd (1951–) starred in the 1970s hit TV show *Charlie's Angels* and appeared in Hollywood movies, including *Purple Hearts*, *Millennium*, and *Permanent Midnight*. She was born in Huron.

François de La Vérendrye (1715–1794) and **Louis-Joseph de La Vérendrye (1717–1761)** were the first Europeans known to have entered today's South Dakota. Two metal plates they left during their travels were discovered in the 20th century.

Ernest Lawrence (1901–1958), born in Canton, won the Nobel Prize in Physics in 1939 and worked on the Manhattan Project, the U.S. government program that created the first atomic bomb.

Manuel Lisa See page 40.

Cheryl Ladd

George McGovern

Cliff Lyons (1901–1974), a native of Lake County, was a Hollywood stuntman for nearly 50 years, filling in for cowboy stars such as John Wayne, Tom Mix, and Buck Jones.

George McGovern (1922–2012) was born in Avon, fought in World War II, and then became a U.S. representative, a U.S. senator, and the Democratic candidate for president in 1972. During his career, he stressed social and economic reforms and spoke out strongly against the Vietnam War.

Russell Means See page 66.

Oscar Micheaux See page 80.

Billy Mills See page 81.

Allen Neuharth (1924–2013) started his journalism career in South Dakota before becoming president of Gannett, a large newspaper company. There he created *USA Today*, the first national newspaper designed to cover general news across the country. He was from Eureka.

Richard Franklin Pettigrew (1848–1926) came to South Dakota to work for the U.S. government. He entered politics and in 1889 was elected one of South Dakota's first two U.S. senators. His home in Sioux Falls is open to the public.

Gladys Pyle (1890–1989), the daughter of Mamie Shields Pyle, was the first woman elected to the South Dakota legislature. She also briefly represented her home state by appointment in the U.S. Senate.

Mamie Shields Pyle See page 56.

Red Cloud (1822–1909) was a Lakota leader who fought to keep white settlers off Sioux lands for several years. In 1876, he chose not to fight, arguing instead that Native Americans should have more control of reservations.

Ben Reifel See page 90.

O. E. Rolvaag (1876–1931), a Norwegian immigrant, was one of the first U.S. writers to use South Dakota as a setting for his novels. His most notable work is *Giants in the Earth: A Saga of the Prairie*.

T. Denny Sanford See page 101.

Billy Mills

Sitting Bull See page 48.

Virginia Driving Hawk Sneve (1933–), a Lakota Sioux author, has written books for both children and adults. Her works include *Enduring Wisdom: Sayings from Native Americans.*

Jess Thomas (1927–1993), born in Hot Springs, was an opera singer who starred in performances throughout North America and Europe. He is best known for the many roles he played at the Metropolitan Opera in New York City.

John Thune (1961–), born in Murdo, was elected a U.S. senator from South Dakota in 2004 and reelected in 2010. Previously, he had served in the U.S. House of Representatives from 1997 to 2003.

Casey Tibbs (1929–1990), who was born in a log cabin near Fort Pierre, became the first great professional rodeo champion, winning the national title for riding a bronco with a saddle six years in a row.

John Blair Smith Todd See page 42.

Touch the Clouds (c. 1838–1905) was a Lakota Indian leader known for his bravery and diplomatic skills. He fought to preserve the traditional way of life of the Lakota people.

Adam Vinatieri

Adam Vinatieri (1972–) is a professional football player who was born in Yankton. He became a kicker for the South Dakota State University football team and then moved on to the National Football League.

Laura Ingalls Wilder See page 78.

Fee Lee Wong See page 50.

York See page 38.

Korczak Ziolkowski (1908–1982) was an artist who won a prize for a sculpture at the 1939 world's fair and then received an invitation to come to the Black Hills and carve an image of the Lakota leader Crazy Horse out of rock. He spent the second half of his life in South Dakota.

Zitkala-Sa (Gertrude Simmons Bonnin) (1876–1938), the daughter of a white father and Dakota Sioux mother, was a writer whose books focus on Indian legends and stories as well as her experiences as a Native American.

Korczak Ziolkowski

Zitkala-Sa

RESOURCES

★ ★ ★

BOOKS

Nonfiction

Gondosch, Linda. *Where Did Sacagawea Join the Corps of Discovery? And Other Questions About the Lewis and Clark Expedition*. Minneapolis, Minn.: Lerner, 2011.

Patrick, Jean L. S. *Face to Face with Mount Rushmore*. Keystone, S.C.: Mount Rushmore Historical Association, 2008.

Petersen, Christine. *South Dakota Past and Present*. New York: Rosen Central, 2010.

Rzeczkowski, Frank. *The Lakota Sioux*. New York: Chelsea House, 2011.

Santella, Andrew. *The French and Indian War*. New York: Children's Press, 2012.

Stanley, George Edward. *Sitting Bull: Great Sioux Hero*. New York: Sterling, 2010.

Straub, Patrick. *It Happened in South Dakota: Remarkable Events That Shaped History*. Guilford, Conn.: Globe Pequot, 2010.

VanEpps-Taylor, Betti. *Forgotten Lives: African Americans in South Dakota*. Pierre: South Dakota State Historical Society Press, 2008.

Zimmerman, Dwight Jon. *Saga of the Sioux. An Adaptation from Dee Brown's Bury My Heart at Wounded Knee*. New York: Henry Holt and Company, 2011.

Fiction

Arrington, Frances. *Prairie Whispers*. New York: Puffin Books, 2005.

Sneve, Virginia Driving Hawk. *Enduring Wisdom: Sayings from Native Americans*. New York: Holiday House, 2003.

Sneve, Virginia Driving Hawk. *Jimmy Yellow Hawk*. New York: Holiday House, 1977.

Wilder, Laura Ingalls. *By the Shores of Silver Lake*. New York: HarperCollins, 2008.

Wilder, Laura Ingalls. *The Long Winter*. New York: HarperCollins, 2008.

Visit this Scholastic Web site for more information on South Dakota:
www.factsfornow.scholastic.com
Enter the keywords **South Dakota**

AUTHOR'S TIPS AND SOURCE NOTES

★ ★ ★

I read many books while doing research for this book. Particularly helpful was *A New South Dakota History*, which features chapters by a variety of South Dakota writers as well as scholars from nearby states. Herbert Schell wrote a detailed history of the state, *History of South Dakota*, which was updated by John E. Miller. To understand South Dakota's geography, I turned to *The Geography of South Dakota* by Edward Patrick Hogan and Erin Hogan Fouberg. Guy Gibbon's *The Sioux* gives both historical and recent information on the Lakota, Nakota, and Dakota Sioux. And *South Dakota*, written by state resident T. D. Griffith, provided useful information on events and sites throughout the state. The state of South Dakota's Web site and the sites for two newspapers, the *Argus Leader* and the *Rapid City Journal*, were essential for information on the state government, economy, and current affairs.